Prelude

Anastasia Watkins was very young when the first abortion bans swept across the country. She remembers her mother and her mother's friends were outraged and she watched as they fought back for women's right to choose. As a teenager she heard the stories about women dying of infection and the chaos and news stories surrounding babies and women dying at alarming numbers in the US.

Then the workplace issues began. Women were forced out of top-level positions in companies and lawsuits were abundant. This began the interest in law for Anastasia. She was taught by her mother to "do something" to make a change when it was clear it was needed.

There were more crooked judges in the judicial system and stories of judges "influenced by wealthy donors" were increasing. Some women in politics were harassed to the point that many dropped out of races due to death threats and women of power were shunned. Women were becoming more outraged each year and there was an underlying movement of women talking and planning and trying to create change.

Anastasia managed to secure her law degree and master's degree in political science and landed a job as the District Attorney of Atlanta Georgia. She was watching the world around her crumble, and she was determined to find other women to help her change the world.

This is the story of her rise to power and her influence on angry women everywhere. It will take years and many close friends and alliances to make the world a better place. Anastasia is certain of her path and determined to make a difference. With the help from her friends, she does just that.

Women everywhere should rejoice in the accomplishments that we have achieved over the past century. This story is just a reminder of how far we have come, and yet, how steadfast we must be, to continue to move forward. Here are just a few things to recall that women fought hard for:

- 1848 - The Seneca Falls Convention (women described grievances about being unable to vote, having no voice in creating laws, and that they had no property rights; resolutions were passed including a right to vote)
- 1913 – Women's Suffrage Parade in Washington (5000 women marched and demanded the right to vote in all states without prejudice)
- 1916 - The first woman was elected to Congress
- 1920 – The 19th Amendment declares woman can vote

- 1923 - Equal Rights Amendment passed in Congress (Including the right for women to own property, hold a job, and become educated)
- 1968 – The first Black woman was elected to Congress
- 1984 – The first woman to be on a presidential ticket
- 2016 – The first woman nominated by a major party for President
- 2020 – The first woman elected as Vice President

In the last 100 years, woman have gone from winning the right to vote to serving in some of the highest positions in government.

Progress has been slow and still uneven. Women continue to be underrepresented in political office. But women continue to push forward and make their voices heard.

For my gray-haired lady friends

You know who you are –

I gain my strength from you.   Cindy

Thanks to my niece,

TERI COAN

For the beautiful COVER

<u>CHAPTER ONE</u>

It has been almost 20 years since there was a two-party system in American politics. The world has struggled, but none more than the people of the United States of America. We watched as the masses went crazy and tried to overthrow the government. There were several attempts. Then finally, decisions were made and the then Republican Party was no more. It had been a sad and disturbing time for most American's. Nobody wanted it to come to this but the unfit had taken so much from so many. People stood up, let their voices be heard, and voted most all Republicans out of office.

The Republican Party tried to keep it together. But after twelve years of failed elections and more rioting in the streets the changes came for the people.

Leona Rae Branson was a young woman just getting her master's degree in marketing. Leona began working in Georgia in 2042 at the ripe old age of 24. An ad agency hired her, and she worked tirelessly selling advertisements that would be posted to the web and blasted on electronic signs that were now all the rage in the US. It made driving very difficult, but most people no longer owned a car, so the Uber drivers are the ones suffering from the flashing neon lights. Most are happy to not drive and have grown to appreciate all the various types of public transportation. There used to be a public transport called MARTA in Georgia, but it eventually closed and was replaced by faster train systems and self-driving vehicles that pick up passengers and drop them off once they request a ride from their phone. The new system is called "Auto Drive" and there are thousands of vehicles on miles of railway and computer systems maneuvering around the country. One can actually get an auto-pilot vehicle to drive to another state now. Leona usually begins her week by scheduling appointments, then scheduling car pick-ups from place to place. The "Auto Drive Scheduler" App on a phone makes it easy work. There are no fees for last-minute changes because of the high demand for the cars. It is likely that about 50% of the population is using this for transport these days. One can even schedule a drive-thru along the route to get one's favorite morning coffee.

Leona has met so many interesting businesspeople over the last few years. And by collaborating with the movers and shakers of these businesses she has become well educated about what works and what doesn't. At least from a marketing perspective she has a lot of this figured out. She has learned that most of the successful businesses are owned and managed by women. In fact, the numbers have been increasing substantially over the past decade. There have been awards given and presidential accolades, for many of the top businesswomen that are influencing the way we work, trade and deal in foreign affairs. It was exciting to watch. However, for some reason many of the women encountered are still finding it difficult to get real empowerment in organizations. So, Leona has listened carefully to what they say and watched what they do, and she is seeing a pattern. "I feel like I can be part of making a difference and I must try. I have set out to do so. I guess my friends would say I am a girl on a mission to make a change for womankind."

Leona is sitting in a conference room waiting to interview for the next level sales position at *Rodgers Advertising* and watching the gentleman across the desk as he looks over her Resume'. Mind you, she has worked here for almost five years now and he should know his employee well enough to either promote her or pass her over quickly. Nonetheless, the company required her to go through the interview process just like any other applicant.

"So, you are Miss Leona Rae Branson, are you?" "Worked here some five years I see."

"Yes, Mr. Williams, you are correct." "I am glad to be here."

The interview went on for about an hour and the balding, overweight Manager decided he would give Leona the promotion. He said, "you earned it kiddo", which sounded like she had done a good job walking his dog or something. She had in fact worked her ass off these past years, lots of overtime and Saturdays when needed, and listened to managers making dumb decisions, so she really wanted to move up this ladder, get to the top and fix this mess! Leona knew she could run this place better than any of the previous managers. She just had to make it happen.

She had managed to get the boss to give her a sizeable rise in pay and the title of *Senior Advertising Executive,* which made her happy at the end of the day.

Now it was time to meet up with the girls and celebrate.

Friday was the usual hangout night. They were a group of 29 to 30-year-old women that were all educated, doing well in their careers, and always wanting more. They had bonded after meeting at a social event a few years ago. They were all attending a political fundraiser for the Georgia State Representative Megan Thomas. She had managed to find all the women in business in her district and sent an invite. She was moving up the Congressional ladder and was a force to be reckoned with in both Georgia and Washington DC. That was a moment that changed all their lives. It was something about the way she spoke to the women in the room, she heard them, she was one of them, and she wanted them to help her make a change. They all agreed they wanted to do just that.

Leona's lady friends, Abigale James or Abby, as they call her, and Kendall Otani, are the best of the bunch. Abby works for the Atlanta District Attorney's office and is kicking some butts as a top-notch litigator. Kendall is the sales manager at a women's clothing company that distributes all over the world. Her friends are busy ladies, and they manage to make Friday nights work whenever possible. They usually get in three out of four Friday's a month. They missed last week so tonight it is going to be catch-up time and Leona will share her promotion news!

Abby and Kendall are already there waiting at Mondavi's Italian Restaurant, and they have an outside table so they can people watch. The bartender and owner of the place is Ty Jones, and he always has a table for the girls on Friday's.

"Hi there Ty!" He smiles and those dimples could melt a girl. Too bad he is married to another friend of mine, Leona thought. The two exchanged their usual winks, and he points to the outside table. "Thanks friend!"

Of course, there is already a bottle of their favorite red wine on the table and three beautiful glasses. After group hugs the ladies begin to all speak at once. Finally, Leona can convince them her news must be first on topic. After explaining her promotion and getting cheers to that and after thoroughly discussing the crazy interview process, they move on to other topics.

Kendall has a huge fashion show coming up and she tells her friends all about it and surprises them with tickets in the front row! "This is no simple fashion show, and it is impossible to get invited unless you are someone important", explains Kendall to her buddies. The table of friends are all so excited and thankful and immediately stop and add it to their calendar for next month. They also schedule a car at the same time because they are sure to indulge in a bit of champagne during the event!

"Kendall, you are too much!" says Abby.

"Yes, too much darling," says Leona.

Kendall is a couple of years older than both Leona and Abby and treats them like her little sisters. She likes to encourage them to take risks in life or as she says, "you will not get anywhere if you just sit there thinking about it…" and her friends love her for this. Kendall was born in the UK and moved to Atlanta in her teens. Her accent is mostly gone now, but she can turn up the British yarn when needed. Some would call her snobby, but the friends know how intelligent she is, and beautiful. Her long dark hair is always in a bun or braid for work, but on occasion her friends see her let it down and add a few curls for ladies' nights out. Men seem to fall at her feet when she enters a room, but she is too busy with her fashion shows to think about dating. "Maybe when I am forty, I will find me a rich old man to marry", she says on the regular nights out.

Abby begins to tell the group about her news from the DA's office. Her boss is Anastasia Watkins, and she has been in this position for a few years now. Ms. Watkins is running for Senator this Fall and specifically asked Abigale to be her campaign manager. She offered to continue her salary if she leaves her position and manages her campaign. Abby was so excited she could barely contain herself. Of course, Abby loves her job and is worried about what happens after the campaign. She is set to meet with Anastasia next week and talk about all the details.

"My gosh this is all too much for one Friday night girlfriends!" And the group raised their glasses with "cheers" all around! Ty saw the friends celebrating something, so he brought out a nice tray of Hors D'oeuvres and placed them in the center of the table and said, "on the house ladies!" "Looks like we are celebrating so enjoy these." It was a longer than usual evening for the group of friends but a good time for sure.

Saturday morning came on with a vengeance. Leona thought perhaps she should have slowed down on the red wine last night, but my goodness we all had a lot to celebrate, she thought. It felt like those dreams she had had in her head of being somebody important and making changes in the world were coming to fruition. But something is still missing from the picture. Leona was happy for her friends and for herself. But she wanted so much more.

By getting involved with Anastasia Watkins' campaign and collaborating with her friends, she thought they could all really support someone they believed in and make needed changes on the political scene. We can support women in politics and help them to help us all, she thought.

Leona has followed Anastasia Watkins for a few years. Of course, her friend collaborating closely with her has allowed an inside knowledge of what the lady stands for and how she sees the future. Watkins platform is one of empowering women to move up in politics and be the decision makers. Her stance on not too much government but enough to help the homeless and disabled has made her real. She also has worked tirelessly on environmental issues and immigration policies that are fair for everyone. She believes in shorter congressional terms to allow for new blood when needed. The old farts do not care for that idea, so she runs into a wall on that one. But her natural look, long grey hair, and challenging work out body, all make a statement. She is healthy, happy, and powerful and Leona was thinking she would love nothing more than to help empower more women like herself.

Kendall and Leona both look up to their friend Abby and she seems older than her 29 years of age. Her dirty blonde hair began to turn grey last year, and she just let it go naturally and would have no part in coloring it. They call her a "natural beauty" and she is the kindest person they know. She takes in stray cats and an occasional stray person! Whenever a friend needs a landing spot, she is quick to offer them a place to stay for as long as they need. She says the Congresswoman, her boss, is her muse and she hopes to be like her one day. She wants to help people and be involved in the big decisions put on our politicians. So, understandably, she is thrilled to have the offer to manage her bosses' campaign.

Leona took her usual run around the local park this Saturday morning with a lot on her mind. As she runs, she says she just enjoys the green trees and blue sky and takes in the fresh air. Children are heard playing near the duck-filled pond and parents are gathered to gossip and laugh at their precious little ones. Leona's brain is working overtime thinking about how she can make real changes in the world. She feels determined to make it a better place for her friends' futures. This is the one thing, among many others, that all the friends have in common. Leona is certain they are bonded together with the desire to make the world a better place and she is determined to make it happen.

Kendall is working her usual Saturday at the Buckhead store outside of Atlanta. The prices are high and the latest fashion trends are in high demand. Kendall cannot remember how long it has been since she had a Saturday off work to just do something fun. But she enjoys her work, and the fashion show is going to be a big boost for her career. Many local celebrities and some from other places around the globe will be in attendance. This is her chance to really make a name for herself.

There are three big designers that will be bringing their latest fashions to the show. Kendall has met with each one and is busy coordinating the layout of the runways and all the behind-the-scenes stuff. Since she also studied public speaking, she is well versed in these events. She will be announcing the designers and their designs. Many see Kendall as just a pretty face. She is Hawaiian decent and has the most fascinating face. Her eyes are blue, from her father's side, and her skin is flawless and tanned like her Hawaiian mother. She also wears her hair long and it is so Black friends say it sometimes looks blue. She has a silky way of speaking, and it makes people listen. Some of the elders say she has an "Obama way of talking to people", and for this reason she is in high demand to speak at charity events and every designer showcase.

Kendall is sitting in her studio going over pages of talking points when Anastasia Watkins walks into her office.

"Miss Watkins, I wasn't expecting you."

"Yes, I know. Sorry to interrupt you but I knew you would be here as Abby says you work every Saturday. I was invited to the show, and I plan on attending. I am very excited to see it."

"But that is not why I am here Miss Otani. I have followed your shows, and you are an excellent speaker. I need someone like you to help me with my campaign. Abby mentioned she told you about me putting my hat in the ring this Fall for the Senator seat."

"Yes, ma'am. She did. We are excited to hear the news and I am a big fan of yours!"

Kendall sat there in bewilderment and wasn't quite sure what to think. Then Watkins explained more details about what was coming up and how she wanted Kendall on "the team".

Kendall explained about her show and the DA understood but insisted on almost begging her to come and work with her. She said she would wait to hear from Kendall in the next couple of weeks and they would discuss it in more detail. She then left her card and said to call her any time and they would chat some more.

Kendall suddenly realized she was sitting at her desk and her mouth was wide open. She shut her mouth and swallowed hard. She looked around the empty room as if to find someone to ask if that just happened. Did the District Attorney of Atlanta just walk in and say she wanted to run for the Senate and wanted Kendall to help her write speeches and make appearances with her? Hmm. Sounds interesting, she thought and then got back to work on her fashion show timeline.

Abby was having her usual Sunday brunch with her sister when her phone rang, and it was Kendall. "Hey lady, here with Sis, what is up?"

Kendall began to explain her encounter with Abby's boss yesterday. She asked her to stop by her condo on the way home so they could talk more about it. Abby agreed and said she was going to finish up brunch and would see her friend for a drink right after.

Abby knew better than to elaborate with her younger sister about this news, so she managed to blow it off as a "nothing new" call.

Abby had just been to the hair salon prior to brunch, and her previously high-lighted blonde hair was gone. She told her hair stylist she had so much gray coming in to just make it all gray. Her sister was shocked to see her so "silver", as she said quite loud. Abby quickly said, "it is just gray so get used to it." Abby was taller than her friends at 5'10" and very slender. She had a way with people and was a great speaker and so very organized. Her friends said she was "OCD", and they were always trying to get her to "chill" a bit. This way of doing business had landed her the job in the DA's office a few years ago. She dressed very smartly in tailored suits she bought from Kendall's showroom. Even just eating a Sunday brunch with her sister required a matching skirt, vest and new Vuitton handbag. Her makeup was always perfect, but not too much. She made her presence known when she walked into a courtroom or a restaurant. Her sister loved that about her. The pair finished up lunch and Abby hurried off to meet up with Kendall.

Abby was in her auto-pilot lift when her phone rang, and it was Leona. She thought about not answering but she knew Leona would think that unusual on a Sunday afternoon.

"Hello darling, just finished up brunch with Dee, how are you doing today?"

Leona was calling to chat about her new job duties and just see what her friend had planned for dinner. After a few minutes of chatting, Leona could tell something was up. "Where are you headed now?"

"Oh, Kendall wanted me to stop by for a quick drink. I think she had a question about the fashion show or something. Not sure."

Leona wasn't buying it. She knew the girls would not get together for drinks without inviting her. But she lived by a code that they had all agreed upon years ago. She would not push for information if it wasn't offered. Instead, she said to call her later if they wanted to get together for dinner or something. Abby agreed to that and finished up the call as she arrived at Kendall's place.

The auto-pilot cars were great, but she never understood why they asked if you wanted to add a tip. Who would I be tipping? She never added a tip for the absent driver. So silly, she thought. She wondered if anyone was dumb enough to actually tip a car. It made her laugh a little to herself as she paid and exited the ride.

The automated voice said, "thank you Abigale James, for your service." Abby hated that the car knew her full name and used it. And, if the passenger ever replied to the car would keep talking. It was all a bit too much, she thought. So, without a peep, she hopped out and the car, without a driver, swiftly drove away.

Kendall buzzed her up. Her condo was a high-rise in a wealthy section of Buckhead. There was a door attendant and a restaurant/bar on the first floor where the friends sometimes met for drinks or dinner although it was quite pricey. Abby went up to the 14th floor which was one shy of the penthouse. Kendall was doing well with her business, and she could afford this place, but it was all a bit much for Abby.

Kendall opened the door and grabbed her friend by the arm and looked down the hallway as if to see if anyone was following her. Abby chuckled as she was pulled into the room.

"What the heck, is this some kind of secret mission we are on here? Chill out girlfriend."

"I just didn't know if anyone was around, or whatever, come inside. Sorry."

Kendall had a way with style on every level. She knew fashion, of course. And she also knew how to decorate her home. She loved black and white, so her décor was very minimalist with white leather couches and black end tables. A large glass and metal light hung in the center of the room. One wall was entirely covered with four television screens. They were never on when Abby visited, and she wasn't sure why her friend needed so many screens. But the place was also warm with fresh flowers and fluffy pillows and rugs.

There was a dining room with a table that was eight feet long. It was piled high with clothing sent from various designers.

In the corner was an office with binders in every color and charts with timelines hung on the wall. It was obvious that Kendall took her work home with her.

But fashion was not the topic of the day. Kendall began to explain her visit with Anastasia Watkins. She told her friend the entire story and waited for a response.

"Wow, that is amazing!" Abby thought the idea of them both working on the campaign together would be wonderful. She adored her friend and decided this was excellent news. Abby herself was still mulling over the question posed to her by her boss, and she was not yet certain she was going to say yes. But this was effective in her mind.

"We would be working together like a team; I love the idea." Kendall had so many questions and so did Abby. They really wanted to talk to Leona and bring her into the loop. But as of now Leona was not really a part of this plan.

The friends began to work through a way of getting Leona involved as well. With her just receiving a big promotion, quitting her job might not be the best thing to do. They were not sure how this would all work out, but they needed input from their friend. Together they called Leona and asked her to meet them for dinner. They would eat downstairs at *Turners* (named for Ted Turner) and then would go back upstairs for wine at Kendall's place.

Leona was on board, and she arrived right on time at 5:30pm. At *Turners* the seafood was fantastic, and they ate and chatted but did not bring up the Watkins campaign until later.

Leona could tell something was up, so they didn't waste time on dinner. Once upstairs the two friends began to explain everything.

"I am going to need more wine," said Leona with a big grin. She grabbed a bottle and poured it generously.

The conversation went on for hours about all the things to come and Leona wanted in on the campaigning trail. She just wasn't sure how to proceed.

It was after 10:00pm when Leona and Abby left Kendall's condo. They shared a ride home in an auto-ride. They did not tip the car.

At home Leona could not sleep. Tomorrow was a big day starting her new position. It really was not going to be that much of a difference in her job, but she would have less direct contact with clients and would be more of a manager of a small team of sales reps.

Leona drew a bath and soaked up the heat, slowly sinking deeper into the suds, then finally submersing herself in the hot water. Her mind and body were equally swimming. She tried her best to relax and think of nothing at all for a few moments. After her bath Leona made herself some hot tea, flipped through her email messages and headed to her bed. Tomorrow would be here soon enough, she thought, and she flipped off the light next to the bed and closed her eyes.

The three friends each realized that evening that something big was about to happen in their lives. They could feel it. There was so much more in store for them. They had collectively dreamed of doing great things and changing the world for the better. Now it seemed like the time had arrived. There was a new energy in the air!

Kendall knew this would be her last fashion show for a while. Maybe the last one ever. She was so excited thinking about working on the campaign. She loved the idea of speaking and writing speeches for Anastasia. She closed the fashion page she was working on and began to google Anastasia Watkins, DA – Georgia – US.

Anastasia Watkins – *Currently serving her third year as District Attorney, Fulton County, GA.*

Middle of the road liberal with sights on environmental protection and immigration rights and services. Tough on crime. Supports women in business. Listed in the "Up and Coming" and "Women to Watch" by Washington DC Journal.

Watkins rallies for protection of women at work and supports woman's rights and women in leadership roles. Known for her long grey hair and big smile, she commands attention when working for a worthy cause.

Called a "natural beauty both inside and out" by her peers.

Kendall read enough and made up her mind that she would meet with the soon to be Senator to discuss plans to get her elected. She would commit 100% as soon as the fashion show was completed and behind her. She will call Ms. Watkins this week and make plans to meet with her soon. And now she would try to sleep.

CHAPTER TWO

It has been three weeks since Kendall, Abby and Leona began talking about working on the campaign of the current Georgia District Attorney, Anastasia Watkins. During this time, the trio of well-educated and empowered women have all had individual meetings with Anastasia.

They came to an agreement that the three women would manage the campaign to include travel, budgets, fundraising, marketing and everything needed to get her elected to the Senate seat that was being vacated this year.

The candidate had plenty of money to get her campaign off the ground as she came from a family that had Texas oil money. The Jefferson family had settled in Atlanta several years ago and Anastasia met and married Hank Watkins two years ago. Hank also came from a wealthy and politically influential family and had grown up in Atlanta and studied Law at University of Georgia. Hank Watkins currently works for a private law group and is working his way up the ladder towards a partnership. His family has many connections with the Democratic party in Georgia and in Washington DC. Hank also has one of those charming smiles and firm handshakes that politicians adore. He personally has not shown much of an interest in holding any office, to the regret of his family. But having a wife that is the current District Attorney and more than ready to throw her hat into the political ring makes Hanks' parents very excited!

The Watkins family met the Jefferson family at their wedding two years ago. Since then, there have been other family gatherings and birthday celebrations shared by the two families that have brought them all closer together. Hank and Anastasia have been talking nonstop about how to get the Senate campaign off the ground. Both families put ideas on the table, and it was finally decided to hold a private dinner party to make the official announcement. Invites will go out to only the topmost elite in the Georgia political arena and a few good friends and business partners that the group knew would offer financial support for the campaign. The date was set for the big event to take place.

June 2nd, a Saturday evening, at 6:30 pm was the date they chose. The dinner would be at the Watkins home in Buckhead. Mrs. Briana Watkins was an expert at hosting such parties and her large extravagant home would be a great backdrop and could manage a crowd of fifty or more guests.

Leona collected her final paycheck from her marketing job and promised to return if this political gig did not go as expected. Her team at the office were happy for her and wished her luck in the new adventure.

Abigale James also was forced to give notice to the DA's office, although she was continuing her relationship with Anastasia, she had to walk away from her current position. Abby, as known by all her friends and colleagues, was a force of her own in the DA office. Any attorneys in town that tried to bully her quickly found out that was not possible. The woman managed her boss's calendar and kept the office running like clockwork. Most co-workers could not imagine the place running without Abby at the helm, but they were about to find out soon enough.

Kendall was finding it more difficult to leave the Boutique. The fashion show was that week and once that was completed, she had to walk away. She knew in her heart that fashion would always play a role in her life, and it was something she would never give up on. She also loved speaking events and was extremely excited albeit a bit nervous thinking about what lay ahead of her on the campaign trail.

Anastasia and Hank, along with both sets of parents, and the campaign management group of women she had hired, all sat down to plan out the dinner event. They met at Hanks parents' home, since this is where the event would be taking place in a few weeks. The team got the lay of the land and decided upon the flow for the event. There would be a small orchestra playing in the garden and hors d'oeuvres and drinks would be passed by a catering group that Mrs. Watkins has used many times.

Just prior to dinner, the group will be called into the conservatory where Anastasia will thank everyone for coming and make her official announcement for the Senate seat.

Dinner will be set up with round tables for some 60 people and each group will be arranged to make for good conversations.

After dinner, a final announcement will be made by the hosts about the upcoming election and how much they would appreciate donations to aid with the campaign and marketing efforts. Each guest will be provided with a card that has their name printed on it and an envelope attached. They will be asked to enter a donation amount and drop the envelope in a box on the way out. Abigale, Kendall and Leona will be introduced as these ladies will be in touch with those in attendance regarding donations and upcoming future campaign events.

Everything was planned out and now they just needed to implement. This was going to be quite a task, but these women were more than ready. They were all quite filled with enthusiasm and excitement.

The friends met a few days later to go over plans and discuss important items like fashion, and hairstyles and where to get a good facial! They laughed and made plans day by day and worked well into many evenings leading up to the big event. The seating chart became an ongoing struggle with both Anastasia and Hank chipping in to make sure they put the right couples together. There were a few that would be competitive about donations and Hank knew who would want to outbid the others.

Leona had plenty of marketing ideas. She had already met with several movers and shakers in the marketing world. She had a deal set with a large group that owned the auto-drive vehicles that rode passengers around the Atlanta area. They reached an agreement to have the car make a short statement from Anastasia Watkins just before the passenger arrived at their destination.

The car auto voice would say *"Your local District Attorney, Anastasia Watkins, would like to thank you for taking this ride and would appreciate your vote for state Senator on November 5th. - stay safe out there."*

Leona explained it all to Anastasia and she thought it was genius! But she said she would like it to be *her* own voice making the statement, if that was possible. "But of course – even more genius!", said Leona to her new boss. Now to get to work on making that happen.

There were other billboard ideas and the usual television appearances, but Anastasia liked the idea of meeting everyday people on the street. So, several places were mapped out for lunches, park visits, hospital visits, and other pop-in visits that would get the attention of the people and the local news stations.

The one thing that kept creeping into the campaign discussions was the opponent that insisted that a woman Senator would be weaker than him and not be able to keep pace with the "men on the hill". This infuriated Anastasia and it just made her work that much harder to get elected.

Meanwhile in the rest of the world the political arena was on fire. Women in every jurisdiction were madder than ever about the direction our country had been going these last few years.

Women had been losing rights and privileges for years and it seemed as though things were moving in the wrong direction. There was now only one woman on the Supreme Court, and she barely made a difference. Many women CEOs had been replaced in recent years and more women were opting to stay home and raise their children instead of sending them to daycare. Work environments had become so extreme and harsh for many women that they were just giving up and throwing in the towel, so to speak.

The school systems have been taking a terrible beating and the funding was lacking to support change. So many teachers have been lost and school violence has been increasing, causing parents to do more home-schooling. There had been bills sent to congress that got shot down by the *old white men on the hill*. This is what Anastasia called the group of older, out of date, Senators that needed to be voted out. It wasn't so much their physical age that was the problem, but many of them were just out of touch with current affairs, and some of them urged on the old-fashioned politics of the 2020's.

There recently was a company that decided to layoff all the women workers and insisted they home-school their children. If they had no children, they were encouraged to do volunteer work and provide support for their spouse. This caused a huge lawsuit of course and it has been the never-ending court case of the era. The men running the sportswear company have been pounding their chest and trying to explain how this is the "way of the future", while riots and picketing takes place outside the corporate headquarters in Utah.

It is obvious, or so many thought, that the company would go under. But it has not gone under, and in fact, many conservatives are supporting the company's philosophy and letting the men run the company and have the women back in the home making dinner and schooling the children. Anastasia and her team think it is all nonsense and she has a huge support group that agrees with her that something must change.

"Watkins for Women" – "Change is Coming"

The new campaign slogans have picked up speed in recent weeks. Donations are coming in at a rapid pace, and even the Watkins and Jefferson families cannot believe the success they are having with fundraising.

Both families are reaching out to donors and doing whatever is needed to support Anastasia for Senator. Anastasia has been busy making her rounds, attending luncheons and dinners and shaking lots of hands. She is tired but continues to move forward. She wants this more than ever.

Anastasia called her team of women together for a special dinner at her home. Hank has plans to be out of town for a couple of days, so she takes the opportunity to bring her girls over for a nice thank you dinner.

Anastasia and Hank live just outside of the Buckhead area in Marietta. Although they make a nice paycheck between them, they have a modest house that sits on a quiet street near a local park. They have no children but do have two golden retrievers named Ruth and Bader. Anastasia planned on a third dog to name her Ginsburg, but Hank drew the line at two. They were both so busy they could barely take care of two dogs as it was.

Anastasia introduced her girls to the women when they arrived for dinner. They had a nice laugh about their names and the dogs loved all the attention. They all sat outside under the pergola having a glass of wine and just talking about work. Then Anastasia asked them to talk about something else. "Can you ladies just fill me in on your lives right now? What is going on with you and your family? What is new besides the campaign work?"

The friends were happy to share the latest gossip and talk about shopping, diets, and dogs. Kendall told the group how she had met an interesting man in her building that walked his golden-doodle every morning. She found herself making plans to arrive at the front of the building just at the same time so she could say "hello" and be on her way. The group laughed and were curious to hear more about the mystery man, but Kendall wasn't ready to share too many details just yet. She did say he was at least six feet tall or maybe taller and had a keen sense of fashion. She described the clothes he wore and how she could tell a man's personality by the shoes he wore. His shoes were impeccable and always clean. He had a nice big grin and perfect white teeth. And he had stopped once to introduce his dog, Joe.

Well, "he sounds wonderful", said Anastasia. There were many more questions, but Kendall quickly changed the subject to Abby and asked her what had happened on her recent date.

"Date?" Leona and Anastasia chimed in at the same time. "Since when do you have time for a date anyway" said Leona to her dear friend.

Abby was quick to respond that it was about fundraising for the campaign. But she admitted that she had told Kendall how this unnamed man had made her blush when he told her how beautiful she was. Anastasia had to hear more about this guy and asked "well, give up the goods – details please!"

Abby spent the next twenty minutes rambling on about Noah Constantine, the art museum Gallery Director, in downtown Atlanta. She had set up a lunch to meet with Noah and discuss a campaign event at his gallery. They ended up having a two-hour lunch followed by a trip to see the gallery that lasted another two hours and then he asked her to go to dinner with him this weekend.

Abby was obviously smitten with this Noah fellow and her friends went on and on with questions and observations. Finally, Anastasia told the group that dinner was ready. They made their way to the dining room that was large enough to seat about twenty people. But it was casual with neutral tones and modern art. It was a happy room that was made for a relaxing dinner. Kendall raved about the fashion designs that Anastasia had chosen. Dark green embossed paper on the dining room walls with crystal sconces set the tone for relaxation in style. And the group did just that. They relaxed and laughed and talked about dating and the future. It was a well-needed easy evening after the last few weeks of work.

Anastasia was so happy to have this powerful group of women sitting in her home. She was more enthusiastic than ever about her future and what it held. She felt certain she could succeed at anything with this smart group of women in her circle. It was a pleasant and satisfying evening for each of them.

They finally got around to talking a bit about the next few weeks and months. The donor dinner was next weekend. Everyone was ready. Anastasia thanked her guests for all they had done already. She was sincere and honest with them about her expectations and what she wanted to carry out with her Senate job. There was so much change that was needed in the world and especially here in the US and in Georgia. Their state had been hit hard with voter fraud accusations several years ago and while they managed to put a lot of politicians in prison over the ordeal, the state had spent a lot of time and money defending itself and trying to get the corruption out of the state. They were making headway, but it had been a tough decade.

Anastasia explained how she needed her close circle to move forward with caution. There were those in politics that were not "good humans" as she would call them. "Ladies, there is evil all around us and we must be diligent in moving forward to change the world", she said.

They promised then and there to do everything in their power, and within the limits of the law, to get her elected to the Senate. And then, they would continue to work for the good of the people to make good, honest, moral decisions that would elevate strong women into positions of power. They took their own "oath" of sorts while sitting at that dining table on that evening. They each understood what they were doing and how they agreed to hold one another up for the good of themselves and for every woman and girl following in their footsteps.

They had a sisterhood of sorts. They had a leader, and they had a team that brought wisdom and strength to the table. Nothing would stop them now.

They were the new society. One day they would rule the world.

The dinner ended with a "cheers to women everywhere" and "cheers to Senator Watkins" and "cheers to us!"

There were hugs all around. And then Anastasia did something unexpected. She wanted her team to know what they meant to her. She handed each one of them an envelope and told them to read it when they got home.

She thanked them again "for everything" and they all said their goodnights. Then without warning Ruth and Bader came bouncing towards the front door to bid the guests a goodnight. The dogs jumped up on each lady and gave them splendid kisses. All the while, Anastasia was demanding they "sit" and "behave", but no matter, it was a perfect goodnight kiss. "Bye now ladies, and thanks for being you!" "Goodnight!"

CHAPTER THREE

Each friend had come separately to the dinner party. Kendall had an auto-pilot car awaiting her while Abby and Leona each drove their own car.

They made their way home without reading the letter or whatever was inside the envelope that Anastasia had handed them.

Kendall arrived at her condo, and it just so happened that Joe, the goldendoodle, and his master were coming up the walkway. The pair paused when they saw Kendall exiting the vehicle. "Oh, hey there neighbor", said the tall handsome stranger. The dog barked as if to also say hello.

"Hi there – Hi Joe"

"So how are you doing on this fine evening, Miss? I am sorry I did not get your name the last time we bumped into each other."

"That's because I didn't give you my name. But I shall. It is Kendall. Kendall Otana. And you would be….?"

"Oh, Uh, sorry about that. This is Joe and I am Oliver. My friends call me Chad." "I know, weird, but my full name is Oliver Chadsworth Turner, so Chad is it. Call me Chad."

Kendall thought it was amusing that Chad was stumbling over his own name. She found it cute and charming.

Chad then went on about walking the dog and where he worked and so on and Kendall just stood there listening to him and not really hearing a word. Finally, she said she had to get inside and would like to chat more with him later.

Chad promptly handed her a business card from his jacket pocket and said, "please call me sometime and we can continue our conversation, if that is okay with you."

"Well, sure. I will do that. Nice to meet you Chad and Joe, of course. Have a good evening neighbor. Goodnight!"

As much as Kendall was really interested in talking more with Chadsworth she had other business on her mind tonight. She could not wait to open the envelope from Anastasia and see what it held.

Kendall went up to her home and slid into her robe and slippers. She pulled her long hair up into a ponytail and opened the envelope as she plopped onto her sofa.

Inside were two items. One was a handwritten letter from Anastasia and the other was a personal check for $100,000.

Kendall began to read the note.

Dear Kendall,

I want to thank you for all you have done for me to date. You have been a good friend and political ally and supported me without hesitation. For this I will be forever grateful.

I have a large inheritance and I can think of no better way to say thank you and to ask for your continued support. This money is not meant to buy your loyalty in any way. It is meant only to help you since I did ask you to quit your job and come on the campaign trail with me.

You may do whatever you wish with the money. I expect you to do something fun or pay off a bill or maybe take a vacation one day. It doesn't matter what you use it for. Just never feel you need to repay me in any way.

I love you as a friend and appreciate you as a business partner. We are on the path to greatness, and I know we can change the world!

Always in your corner, Anastasia

Kendal sat there with tears in her eyes. Why was she crying? Someone just handed her a hundred thousand dollars! Oh, my goodness, she thought, what in the world just happened?

She sat quietly and thought about what this meant. Why did she do this? What is the real motivation here? Lots of unanswered questions were running through her mind. Finally, she came to the realization that the lady has tons of money and it meant very little to her so if she could share some of it and make someone else's life better than she should do that. It makes sense that Anastasia would think like this.

Kendall had heard from the newswire that the Watkins family had so much money they could buy their way into politics. They wrote that money could pay for the Senate seat. But that is not what Anastasia is about. She would give all her money away if she could just make the world a better place. In fact, she is known for her huge contributions to environmental projects and other charity projects. It is just who she is.

What a nice thing to do. And yes, it does feel like some added pressure to do the right thing and work harder for her new almost Senator. For now, she decided to put the money into her savings, maybe splurge on a few new outfits or shoes, then worry about it all later. She liked this new friend of hers and no doubt they would definitely be making some changes.

Leona arrived at home and immediately opened the envelope. She could not believe what she was seeing. $100,000 check payable to her. For what, she thought?

Dear Leona,

I am so happy to have you on my team! I want you to know how much I appreciate you and all your talents. I can share this wealth with you and your teammates, my friends, and so I am. No strings attached. This is just a thank you for a job well done. You have given up everything, including a big promotion, to come and work with me. I can never repay your loyalty and am forever grateful.

Please do what you wish with the money. I have given the same to each of you on my team. I want you to know how valuable you are to my campaign and to our future.

Together we will do great things. Just wait and see! Now let us get out there and change the world for the better. I know we can do it.

Always in your corner, Anastasia

Leona was in disbelief. Was this happening? She thought about calling her friends, but she knew they were also trying to process this. It would take time to understand why Anastasia did this. But Leona knew it was mostly because she could.

Leona was happy to use some of the money to pay off student loans and pay off her car. This would help her tremendously and take those burdens off her. She could not thank Anastasia enough for her kindness.

She sat down at her desk and began to write out a thoughtful *Thank You* letter to Anastasia. She cried tears of joy as she wrote her kind words.

Abby was at home and had been pondering the envelope, half afraid to open it. She poured a glass of wine and took a hot bath. She thought about what could be inside the envelope and made herself crazy before deciding to just open it.

Dearest Abigale,

You have been such a great support to me over the past few years. I have grown so close to you and am glad to call you my friend.

You know of my inheritance and how this money means so little to me, other than being able to use it to help others. I just want to provide some help since you have given up so much trying to help me. I am stronger with you by my side. I would not have the courage to run for office without your support and trust.

So, take this money, never think about thanking me or paying it back, please. It is yours to do what you wish. It is my <u>thank you</u> bonus!

I am so happy to have your team of friends in my corner on this journey. I just know we have great *things ahead of us and we will make a change. A change is needed. For the world, for women everywhere, for our neighbors and friends, it is for them that we serve.*

Forever in your corner, Anastasia

Abby was overwhelmed by the words from her friend. This was too much, she thought. She had to pick up the phone and call Leona and Kendall. She got them both on the line and there was silence at first. Then, suddenly, they each screamed like schoolgirls! They were all talking at once.

"Oh my God!"

"What just happened!"

"Are you kidding me?"

Then they quietly began to discuss the situation. They were all in agreement that there was no underlying message here. It was who Anastasia Watkins was. She was kind. She was giving. She wanted to say thank you in a big way, so she did. It was amazing and they would never forget her kindness. They each felt comfort in the direction life was moving forward.

"Tomorrow is a new day ladies, a great big new day for all of us and for our futures." Abby said, "love you both" and "good night" then hung up the phone and headed to bed. What a day it had been. What could top this tomorrow, she thought.

CHAPTER FOUR

It was the night of the big event. The donor arty was on. Everything was set up and double-checked by Mrs. Watkins, the Mother-in-Law of Anastasia (Jefferson) Watkins.

Guests began to arrive at the Watkins residence in Buckhead, just outside of the city of Atlanta. Buckhead is well known for the wealth and star quality of some of the residents. Many famous musicians and artists live in the area and the homes are quite opulent.

Leona arrives and is greeted by the Valet. There are red velvet ropes strung up the long curved front drive. Leona makes her way into the home and is greeted by Mrs. Watkins. Mr. Watkins is nearby shaking hands with the mayor. Hank suddenly appears and says that Anastasia has been looking for her.

"Please come this way, Anastasia is upstairs waiting for you all to get here. She is a nervous wreck tonight."

Hank pulled Leona along and up the grand staircase in the center of the foyer that was now crowded with incoming guests. They made their way to a bedroom at the end of the long hallway. Leona was wondering just how many bedrooms this house must have. Maybe six or more? There seemed to be doors forever in that hall.

Finally at their destination Hank knocked loudly, shoved Leona into the room and made his escape. "Here is your friend!", and Hank told her "Good luck!"

Abby was inside sitting on a loveseat next to Anastasia and they were chatting quietly and toasting with a glass of champaign. Leona was glad to see that Anastasia was not "a wreck" as Hank had said moments ago in the hallway.

"Oh, there you are", cried Anastasia, and she told her friend to "sit dear", "we are toasting to a lovely evening with no drama!"

"Now where is Kendall? Have you seen her?"

"No, not yet, but I just walked in myself. I barely had time to say hello to your mother-in-law before Hank whisked me away." "There is quite a crowd gathering downstairs. Is it just sixty guests, because it looks like a hundred!"

"My mother said it was more like sixty-eight if everyone showed up." Anastasia seemed calm and in good spirits. She looked amazing in her black velvet pants suit with silk cuffs. Her long gray hair was braided and pinned up in back with a rhinestone comb pushed into one side. Very sophisticated looking for the next Senator, if things go our way, thought Leona.

Just then the door opened, and Kendall walked in wearing a long black dress that most likely came right off the rack from her recent fashion show. The back swagged down quite low and was trimmed in pearls. It was quite an eye catcher for sure. Her long blue-black silky hair was pulled to one side to not cover her backless dress, which was the star of the show tonight!

All the ladies at once said "Wow!" "Now that is a dress." The friends all complemented one another on their fashion choices. It had been decided earlier that the entire team would wear black tonight. Anastasia was the only one in pants while the rest of the group wore dresses. All the attire was chosen by

Kendall of course. She even managed to dress Hank and found dresses for both mothers in attendance.

As planned the guests had been escorted into the garden. It was a perfect late summer evening, and the large oak trees made a nice canopy over the garden. Of course, Mrs. Watkins added a large white tent with air conditioning, so her guests did not have to endure the Atlanta heat. Twinkling lights lit up the massive oaks and lit the entire backyard. It was magical to see!

The Watkins and Jeffersons made their speeches and thanked everyone for coming. Anastasia stood up in the dining room just before the dinner was served and made her speech. It was perfectly executed as planned. She got a standing ovation with much applause. She smiled a huge smile and instructed everyone to enjoy their dinner.

The dining room was the home's over-sized conservatory. It could host over a hundred people and on this night, it seated sixty. There were a handful of last-minute regrets. But the room was full, and the décor was amazing. So many beautiful tropical plants, an abundance of candles and lots of natural light coming through the all glass enclosure. It was a sight to behold as the sun was setting.

At the end of dinner Hank made a few jokes, and the guests found him quite funny, then he introduced his wife again for some comments. She brought her team up front with her and introduced each lady and said some wonderful things about them. It was obvious that they were a team of four beautiful, intelligent, enthusiastic young women and everyone there was eating out of their hands in that moment. Now they just had to get those donations and keep the momentum going!

At the end of the night, when all the guests had left, the team of four women gathered in the library. Anastasia said to them again, "thank you each so much for everything. Now that is enough for one day so get home and relax for the weekend. I will see you on Monday and we will begin to change the world!"

Leona began to say something, and Anastasia cut her off. "Nope, not a word. Go home."

She knew they wanted to talk about the money and say thank you. But Anastasia did not want to make it a big deal. It was done. Time to move on. So, they did.

Monday came soon enough, and the team gathered at the campaign headquarters for their usual Monday morning meeting. The plans were set for the next three weeks. Before they could end the meeting, the phones began to ring. The donors at the dinner party had been busy already reaching out to friends and businesses and the callers were wanting to donate or offer to help with campaigning.

Anastasia headed out on a road trip with Hank and the friends were left to man the shop. More people were coming to help with the phones and to go out in the neighborhood and talk to people about their future Senator. It was a busy few weeks and the money was rolling in for the Watkins team.

The opposition was understandably angry and began to put together the usual negative advertising. They tried the adage about women being unable to lead in politics and that landed flat with most folks. Anastasia Watkins on the other hand found large groups gathering any time she stopped in a town, and she was in high demand for townhall meetings and luncheons. She spoke with power and enthusiasm about women's rights and how men had been less than understanding about how to deal with the crisis in America. There were school and work issues and daycare and healthcare issues. These things had been ignored for too long. Women everywhere were taking note of what was happening in Georgia. There was suddenly a flurry of activity, and groups were forming around the country to support the Georgia Senatorial race. This was not just about Georgia anymore. It was across the US that women were voicing their opinions, and they were becoming more enraged about how things had gone from bad to worse over the last twenty years.

Women from all states were out meeting with their local leaders asking questions and wanting to hear their opinions on Anastasia Watkins. What did they think? Did they agree? They wanted answers and they were only getting lip service.

As they got closer to election time the rallies were bigger and the message more intense. The group of women on the Watkins team met often to discuss plans and figure out how to get things done. At one meeting the group decided they needed more than the four of them to be an effective *movement* for change. Who else was out there that could be part of their group or perhaps they needed a more organized group of women across all states that worked as they did as a team. Each state needs their own team, their own Senators and Congresswomen, and local Mayors and Governors. Where had all the women gone? They were just not there. But women everywhere wanted to be in power. They were crying out to be included. They want change. They want a new kind of world.

They do not want to continue this path of moving backwards in time. It must stop, and this group knew it was time to make it happen. But how?

Anastasia told her friends that she needed to get into the Senate seat and then they could really make things happen. "We cannot fight this battle alone and we need some political power."

Anastasia knew this was the first step in solving this problem. There would be hills to climb. This was just the first step in many to make change happen. She rallied her troops again to get out there and help her. And they did.

On November 5th, 2048, Anastasia Jefferson Watkins was elected to the US Senate! She beat her opponent by getting over 50% of the votes. This was the most votes ever registered in Georgia and the most ever in any race for US Senator. The headlines were all about this moment in history and people all over the United States and around the world now knew about Anastasia Watkins, US Senator, from Georgia.

And this was just the beginning!

CHAPTER FIVE

Christmastime is here! Leona loved Christmas more than anything. After the election she had moved to a new home in Marietta Georgia that was close to her family and friends. She was done with living in the city in a condo. So, she bought a house. She was also tired of being alone so on her 30th birthday she got a cat. Cats were easy, she thought. I can leave town for a day and come back, and she will survive. Of course, Cher would survive. Yes, her cat was named "Cher" after the one and only. Besides loving Christmas, Leona loved music from the 80's and 90's and thus her love for the singer, Cher!

Her new housemate was all black with one small white patch on her neck. She was stubborn and moody, and Leona adored her new buddy. They spent hours lying on the couch reading the latest political updates. They kept informed and they kept one another company. The relationship worked.

Leona had worked tirelessly on decorating for the holidays. Although the new job was keeping her extremely busy, she just had to make her new home the perfect backdrop for friends to gather and enjoy some holiday wine and Christmas cookies! Leona was a sucker for sweets and had tried her hand at making several kinds of cookies and candies to share with her friends. Outside there was a nice-sized front porch that welcomed her guests, so it was decorated as well. Colorful lights were hung on the railing and oversized fresh greenery was draped around the door and porch posts. Lanterns with candles were next to the glider, and the ladies would spend hours sitting and talking about work and life on that porch. So far, Leona thought, her first Christmas in her new house was quite perfect.

Leona was thrilled to be working in Senator Watkins' office as the Director of Marketing. She had three young students reporting to her that answered phones and emails and kept her informed of any unusual happenings related to the Senator. It was a decent job, and the behind-the-scenes stuff is what kept her there. Many private meetings with members of the new group they amusingly named themselves *The Gray-Haired Women's Club*. Anastasia chose the name because she and several of the other members had gray hair and it was funny. If anyone heard of the club, they would never think it was a political group. The business they discussed was anything but funny or light and it was very political. It was intense discussions around the problems of the day and how to make a change. Leona, Abby and Kendall were all members of the newly formed group, and they enjoyed being involved with these powerful women.

Kendall worked in the office of Senator Watkins as the Finance Manager. Anything having to do with money had to pass through her office for approval. Kendall made sure that part of her duties included keeping the Senator up to date on her fashion style and her bookkeeping. She always found the latest trends and kept Anastasia current. This pleased her and as she said many times to her new boss, it "keeps me sane". She was good with the money issues but loved the fashion world and would never be left behind in the latest movements. She regularly attended fashion shows and would drag her new boyfriend, Chad, along with her.

Kendall remained in her large Buckhead condominium and had begun dating Chad a few months ago. She was going out less with the girls and more often with her new man. Chad seemed to fit for Kendall. He was stylish and what the girls would call fashion forward, with his leather vests and tight slacks. Chad was tall and thin but muscular, so he was the complete package, according to the friend group that was doing the judging.

Tonight is "date night", Kendall told her friends. "Can you believe Chad makes me set dates for the entire month because he says my calendar is so full, he would never see me!" "So, every other Saturday is our date night and there is a penalty to be paid if either of us has to cancel."

The friends found this amusing and probably smart on the part of Chad because he was right. He realized soon in the relationship that Kendall was always "busy" with something. So far, this system has been working for them.

Tonight, they are going to a local Holiday concert that is also a benefit for Congresswoman Megan Thomas. Megan met Chad at his shop when she went to buy a Harley Davidson motorcycle for her husband last month. It is going to be his Christmas present. She was impressed with Chads charm and the way he did business and she invited him to her benefit concert. Of course, Kendall was going to be there, but the Congresswoman was sure to insist Chad join her. It was "black tie" so that meant bringing out the tuxedo! Kendall was nervous about attending the event, but soon realized it was a more laid-back evening of jazz and good food, and of course, fashion! Kendall wasted no time going through the racks of dresses she had access to and finding the perfect one for this event. Red was the color of choice with a black faux fur wrap. Her shoes elevated her 5'10" frame to about 6' which put her at eye level with Chad.

"Wow", he said as he met Kendall at the door. "What did I do to deserve you in my life?"

Kendall blushed a little and the pair headed to his car to make the event on time. It was *Star Studded* and all the who's who of politics were there, including Anastasia Watkins, her boss.

"Hello Kendall", Anastasia said from across the room. "You look fantastic as usual." Immediately she introduced her date, and they made small talk with the Senator before she was pulled away by another more important guest. Kendall and Chad may not have been the most known of guests in attendance, but they were getting some looks. The duo was a sight for sure. Both were quite tall and good looking. Kendall carried herself well and she had a way with words, so speaking to several of the folks in the room was easy for her. Chad, of course, liked to talk about motorcycles so he was able to hold the men's attention at the bar. They managed to mingle well with the crowd and made some new friends.

The evening was wonderful with good wine, good food and some of the best jazz musicians Kendall had ever heard play. She was ready to get out of the tight red dress and get comfortable with her man, so they made their way home.

Tonight, would be spent at Chad's place with Joe. Kendall wasn't sure who she adored more, the boyfriend or his dog. Joe was the sweetest goldendoodle with the best manners. He always greeted them with excitement but was trained to go sit or lay on his bed and not to be a bother. Joe always got extra kisses and belly rubs from Kendall, so he was excited when she visited.

This was not their first rodeo and Kendall asked Chad for a nightshirt she could slip into to so she could be more comfortable. He came from the bedroom with a grin on his face and handed her a tiny cutoff tee shirt and asked if that would be okay. They both laughed and decided no shirt was needed and they made their way to his bedroom.

Chad and Kendall seemed to just fit together easily, and the lovemaking was good. Neither had yet said the "L" word but there was an understanding that this relationship was going somewhere. They held one another close and whispers of things they wanted from one another were exchanged. Every touch brought more heat, and the night was long and hot and perfect. Stress from work and life melted away when they held one another like this. They each knew it was special and they loved this time together. They made love for hours, then they talked and ate a snack and talked some more. Finally, by morning they slept. It was Sunday and they found these to be the most perfect days in their relationship. There were no chores, no projects, and nobody to bother them. It was their world for a day, and they soaked up every moment of it.

Suddenly there was knocking on the door. Neither of them was expecting anyone to visit and it was Sunday late morning, so this was out of the norm. Chad asked Kendall to stay put and he would get the door as Joe began to bark to announce an intruder.

Chad looked out the peephole of the door to see something green that looked like a bush or a tree. He opened the door to find Noah and Abby and Leona holding a Christmas tree.

"Surprise!" The group yelled in unison and Noah drug the 6' live tree into the condo leaving pine needles in a stream on the floor.

"Where shall we put her, asked Noah?"

About that time Kendall appeared from the bedroom laughing at her crazy friends. They had been talking about their own Christmas trees and she had mentioned that Chad did not want the mess of a tree, so he decided not to put one up this year. This was not okay with the group of friends so there they stood, holding the tree, Leona holding boxes of ornaments, and Abby carrying a basket of bagels, fruit and wine!

Kendall looked at Chad as if to say "sorry", but nothing came out of her mouth, besides her big toothy grin. Chad smiled back and they all laughed and went to work finding the tree stand that had been in storage. The friends spent a couple of hours snacking, singing holiday songs and decorating the tree. It was a wonderful Sunday and then came the news Abby was dying to tell her friends. "We are engaged!" Abby yelled the announcement and her friends yelled back in delight and hugs were shared by the group. Noah quickly told them he was picking up her ring tomorrow because it was too big and had to be sized. He had presented the ring Friday night after a romantic dinner, and they spent Saturday visiting family and letting the parents know about their news.

Abby had not wanted the usual diamond ring and Noah knew her all too well by now. So, the ring was a large emerald surrounded by small diamonds. He had also bought matching earrings which she was wearing now. The girl's decided Noah was pretty cool, and he could marry their friend. Now they would have a wedding to plan, along with their busy lives. This would be so much fun, they thought, and the ideas began to take over the conversation.

Abby offered up "there is no set date just yet, but we don't want to wait too long. I don't want him to change his mind you know!"

"Oh, you are all stuck with me. Sorry. Too late now to turn back. I know too much about each one of you, so I am officially on this team!" Noah was so cute, thought all the girls, with his charming smile and the way he looked at their friend. They were a perfect pair.

The tree was successfully decorated, and the food and wine had been shared so the team of friends decided to go their separate ways for the evening.

Chad confessed to Kendall that he thought what the friends did was "pretty cool". He loved the tree, and he loved her and her goofy friends. It was a perfect holiday weekend.

On Monday morning at Senator Watkins' office there was a buzz about new Congressional seats opening in Washington. Since the change in the party system, now called the "Party of Democracy", there have also been changes in various constitutional rules and political timelines. One big change was that the House of Representatives could hold office for 5 years and Congress seats would be for 10 years. There were two openings after the first of the year because two Congresspeople were being forced into retirement. A new rule demanded an independent medical review board must find a person holding office to have sufficient cognitive skills to stay in office. The list was quite long of things they must be able to do and included things like, drive a vehicle, walk without aid (or be in a wheelchair), pass a cognitive skills test and neurological exam. It seems two of the Senators holding seats in Congress did not pass the test and must retire. Since the laws changed some six years ago nobody now questions the testing and members agree to a no-contest ruling.

So, now the question is who gets the seats. There will be a quick election and sitting members will nominate someone, then up to ten names will be given to the panel. The highest-ranking members of Congress along with the Vice President will decide on the new members by February 28th next year. This leaves little time for maneuvering or marketing for the position.

Megan Thomas, Congresswoman from Georgia, was one of the members being removed. She was a fine lady and was in fact recently added as a member of the Gray-Haired Women's Club. Megan was 75 years old and recently was diagnosed with severe rheumatoid arthritis which had caused her to fall a few times at public events. She admittedly suffered great pain in recent months. Rather than indulge the medical panel she volunteered to be removed. Thomas had her mind set on someone she wanted in her place. Anastasia Watkins was the choice, and she sent her name to the committee and asked some of the other members to endorse Anastasia, which they were quick to do. It was beginning to look like Watkins was headed to a Congressional seat in Washington.

The Gray-Haired group planned a special meeting to discuss how to secure this spot for

Anastasia, and what other powerful women they could aid in moving into the other vacant seat.

To keep the woman's group a secret, they had to be very discreet with meetings. Only five or six of the ranking members met in person together and the rest of the group called in on a secure video conference line. The women across America that were part of the movement had reached almost 200 members: 189 at last count. The recent meetings were set up to appear to be holiday gatherings. Christmastime made it easier to cover up gatherings of twenty or so women.

They came from every state in the union except Florida and Louisiana for some reasons that are not entirely clear to Leona. She was the one that tracked all the members, and she kept them all in the loop of upcoming events, meetings, and causes.

What used to be Texas was now Mexicas. In a strange and horrible civil war at the border of Texas and Mexico, a dictator took over, fueled by the Cartel, and overthrew Texas. The states surrounding Texas built tall walls and armed themselves against those trying to flee Texas or Mexico. Texas had no choice but to be taken over by Mexico and try to rebuild the new country. It was a terrible day for the United States and worse for the people of Texas. Many escaped prior to the civil war that broke out, but a lot of Texans were just stuck between the US and Mexico and were forced to stay put.   There were those that were glad to stay and that wanted nothing to do with America. They were glad to leave and build their own country. Most now understand the price they would pay for the so called "freedom from the US laws" and they live in a constant state of turmoil, war and violence. Mexicas is now a new country that is led by a crazy former Texas Governor and his friends in the Cartel. Nobody goes in or out of this new hostile land and it is uncertain what the future will bring for those people.

A few politicians from Mexicas had tried to reach out to the current president, but so far, no world leaders want anything to do with this new country. It is not known what is down the road for those people.

The 189 members of the Gray-Haired Women continues underground and grows steadily day by day, month by month and year by year. These resolute women have managed to bring back some of the women's rights that were stolen during the 2020's. Workers' rights are also making a turn and some Unions are back in the manufacturing arena. Several new women politicians have hosted new bills to find funding for workplace childcare and Medicare has been funded more aggressively than ever to be sure our elderly population is taken care of with certainty. One can feel the change in the air. 2050 is going to be a good year for change! Leona and her friends could see it coming and were proud to be part of something so good and so right and so needed.

The Christmas parties were called Christmas parties again. For at least twenty or more years the entire population was forced to use the words "Holiday" party. Most folks still say this without bother, but many have come back around to calling it whatever they want. It is okay again to just say "Merry Christmas" to a friend on the street or in a restaurant and not feel as though you are breaking the law.

The ladies gathered to plan the wedding of Noah and Abby and they had set a date for next summer. July 30th, 2050, would be the wedding day and Abby had already asked both friends to be her bridesmaids. She had asked Anastasia to be the *Maiden of Honor* and she had accepted without hesitation. Abby had to silently chuckle at the thought of having a Congressperson as her Maid of Honor. Now that was something, she thought to herself.

Wedding planning has changed in recent years. Everything was virtual. Models wore dresses and videos online were viewed by the buyers (the brides to be). A dress could be chosen, sent to the bride, tried on and then returned if she didn't approve. Gone were the days of running from store-to-store spending hours poring through racks of dresses. It was still done by a few, but most preferred the easier virtual viewing experience.

Abby still wanted to do some things the traditional way, so she pushed for an in-person experience. She had other ideas as well and she was so excited to be a bride.

<u>CHAPTER SIX</u>

While the rest of the world may not be paying attention the underground world of powerful women has been hard at work. Three years of meetings, secret promises and due diligence has paid off for the group and society as a whole is winning.

There have been no less than a dozen new women CEOs in businesses across several states, six new political seats taken from men, and more than a dozen new pieces of legislation that give back earning power, medical power and decision making to women. All these things had been stripped from women across the US from 2020 until 2050 when the change became reality.

Now in 2050, there are new medical advances, and some control of the runaway healthcare costs is beginning to show. Most big pharma leaders have been challenged and cuts have been made at the state and federal level to cap drug costs. It helps to have Mexicas wrapped up in their own civil war, so the drugs are not coming out of that area like they used to in years past. The drug Cartel is suffering huge losses, and the US is pushing back on drugs coming into border states.

Anastasia was elected to Congress, and she now has an office in Washington, DC. Her loyal team works for her out of the Georgia office but recently Anastasia asked Abby and Noah to consider moving to Washington this year. Since meeting Abby, Noah has met a lot of people on the political scene and has shown an interest in politics. While he loves the arts and manages a huge gallery in Atlanta, the idea of being in DC close to the action does intrigue both him and Abby. They decided a dinner with friends was in order.

Abby moved from her home in Marietta and she and Noah bought a home in Roswell, just north of the city. Roswell is home to several well-known artists from the Atlanta area and this helped with the decision to live there. They had found a cute craftsman style bungalow and made it pop with art and an eclectic style of furniture. They were proud to entertain themselves there, and this place would be missed if they decided to follow Anastasia to Washington.

Kendal and Chad arrived by auto-driver so they could have drinks and not have to drive home. Leona did the same. She in fact did not own a car and felt it unnecessary.

The purpose of the dinner was somewhat obvious to the group of friends. All that Abby could talk about was the possibility of living in Washington and working there. Her friends were certain this was either an announcement or a quest for information and advice. It turned out to be a little of both.

It was April in Atlanta which meant the weather would either be eighty degrees and sunny or an ice storm. It so happened it was a nice day and not too warm or too cold. Noah set the table on the patio, and they had an outdoor heater on standby if it got too cool. Abby prepared her specialty food item, seafood pasta with salad. She topped it off with fresh baked bread from a nearby bakery, and a nice bottle of white wine. Abby pulled out her nice dishes that she picked up at a local thrift store. And she used her best wine glasses that were a gift from her parents for the engagement party held a few weeks ago.

"Wow, the good stuff" commented Chad and Kendall just smiled at him and winked at Noah.

"Very nice girlfriend" said Leona with a smile. "We must be in for some big news I guess?" Leona gazed at her friend and said, "Let's have it then, what is up with you two?"

Abby did most of the talking and shared what she and Noah had been thinking about for a couple of weeks now. They were leaning towards making the move to DC, but the thought of leaving Atlanta and their dearest friends and business partners was just too much to handle. They could not make this decision without input from the entire group.

Leona went first and offered her advice that included doing "whatever makes you happy". She also explained how they would be in contact regularly due to working with Anastasia. And she personally would love to spend some time in DC, so it seemed like a win-win to her! "You seem to want this very much honey, so I think you just go for it. Now seems to be a good time for a fresh start with your new almost hubby!"

Kendall and Chad chimed in saying pretty much the same as Leona. They were closer to Abby and Noah and had regularly dined out and hung together for most of the political events they attended. Chad seemed to be the most saddened by the current events. He had become very close to Noah and was going to be in the wedding. They were on a softball team together and hung out at the local pub and at the golf course. He didn't want to lose his buddy, but he was having a difficult time coming up with reasons for them to stay in Atlanta.

Kendall smiled at the group and added her thoughts out loud. "You guys will be happy in DC. You will be the new power couple in town." The group cheered at that comment. "Really though, we will miss you terribly, but it just seems right for you. You have our blessings."

Chad added, "yep, I guess you have your answer. Go conquer the world my friends! Cheers to you!" Then he pretended to cry a little which brought laughs from the group at the table.

The group consensus was that they should go if they want to go. Friendships will remain intact wherever they live. Chad even chimed in with "The world is not so big these days when one can hop on a plane and be across the country in a few hours, ya know." "We will figure it out guys." "Go do your thing."

The food was good, and the evening went long so Noah lit the heater on the patio. The group toasted with good wine and a few tears were shed but it ended on a high note. They truly loved one another like family and this bond would last forever. They were sure it would.

Leona arrived home and her sweet kitty, Cher, was waiting at the door. She greeted her with high pitched meows as if to say, "where have you been all night?"

"I know honey, it was a long night. I am sorry you have been alone tonight." "Mommy will give you some belly rubs and tell you all about it. Our friends have some big plans ahead of them and we are going to miss them."

Suddenly, without warning, tears trickled down Leona's cheek. She wasn't sure why, but she was sad. She guessed it was because the life that was comfortable was about to change. One of her best friends was moving away. Too far away to meet up for a quick glass of wine and talk about the crappy day they just had. Too far away for a nice hug or a smile to ease the pain of bad news. Too far away to meet up for dinner or a stroll in the park. It was going to be hard living here without Abby in her daily life. She looked at Cher and asked her "do you need a Sonny?" I thought so. We will find you a friend, a partner, a companion to share things with when I am not around. I promise you."

The kitty meowed at Leona as if she understood her every word. Then she purred as she got the belly rub that was promised her. They lay in the bed and drifted off to sleep.

Kendall and Chad got home and went to Kendall's apartment. Chad explained how his place was a mess and that he had no food or wine there. Kendall was not surprised. It seemed lately they hung out at her place more and more. Chad had even mentioned them moving in together. He said it was silly that they spent so much time together and paid two big mortgages along with all the amenities fees in the building. They both enjoyed the convenience of living in the Buckhead location, but it was very pricey, and Chad was right. They barely visited his house anymore.

So, they talked more about their future. Neither of them wanted to bring up marriage but they did. It had to be said. Kendall started by saying that she wasn't looking for a ring or marriage but wanted them to seem more permanent. "Honey, you know I love you, right?"

Chad responded with "of course I do babe" and he began to shuffle his feet and wrestle something out of his pants pocket.

To Kendall's surprise she was staring at a small velvet box. He held it out and said to her, "My darling, I don't need you to be my wife, but I would like a life partner. And with this ring I promise myself to you for as long as you will have me."

Kendall looked in astonishment at her love. He was standing there holding that box, then he opened it, and inside was the most beautiful gold ring that swirled into a rose. He placed it on her ring finger and said, "I love you."

Kendall began to cry and smile and hugged her man fiercely. "I love you too you knucklehead." She was shaking and holding on to this moment. She wanted to never forget this. Chad scooped her up and carried her into their bedroom and he told her he wanted to show her just how much he loved her. She agreed that would be fine and gave him that big toothy grin of hers.

In the morning Kendall lay next to this perfect man in her bed and wondered what life had in store for her now. She was glad to commit to Chad and they would figure it all out together. She jumped from bed and began to make breakfast. She was humming and cooking as Chad made his way past her for coffee. He looked at his love and had never seen her eyes look so bright and happy. She smiled as he caressed her hips with his free hand. He told her he liked his eggs "over easy please", to which she replied, "anything for you dear", and they laughed together, all smiles and giggles.

Noah and Abby woke up with tired headaches from the hours of talking and decision making the days before. Their friends said exactly what they knew they would say, but they had to hear from them directly. They realized that it was a decision only the two of them could make, but somehow having the support of friends and family made it seem right. Then the phone rang and reality set in. It was Abby's mother. She lived in Alabama and had been in town for the engagement party she planned for her daughter, but she had not been back since then.

"Hello Mom, how are you?" "Oh, really, you want to come for a visit when?" "No, not much is happening here, but I did want to talk to you so this weekend would be fine. We are not too busy."

Noah just looked at her and smiled. "Your mama is not gonna like this one bit you know." "She likes her girl within reach." Then he began to smile and laugh out loud. "Maybe Chad will want to play some golf on Saturday!" He left the room and Abby continued her conversation with her mom.

Mrs. James has been divorced from Abby's father for twenty years. It was just Abby and her mom growing up in Alabama until she left for college and ended up at Georgia Tech studying Marketing and Technology. Abby stayed in Atlanta after college and found her way into the job at the DA's office. She had a minor in Criminal Justice, so the DA office seemed to be a good fit. Her mother, Kristen James, was an artist and musician. She had played cello for the first chair with a local orchestra and worked part-time at an art gallery in Mobile. Noah and her mom had similar art interests, so they hit it off the first time they met last year. In fact, each time Mrs. James came for a visit she would spend hours talking about art with Noah. Abby was slightly jealous of their shared art knowledge, but she was glad her mom approved of her boyfriend, and now fiancé. And she was happy that her mom was coming for a visit.

CHAPTER SEVEN

Sandra James came as promised for a weekend visit with her daughter and the boyfriend.

"Mom, I thought we would visit a local art gallery in town then I picked out a nice place for lunch. Does that sound like fun?"

"Of course it does. You know I am a sucker for any kind of art gallery and Atlanta has the best food places of any city. Sounds like a good plan." "You know how much I miss you sweetie? We don't have to do anything as long as I can see your pretty face and we can catch up on our girl talk. I want to hear more about your new adventures with Ms. Watkins."

The ladies set out for the day, and they enjoyed strolling through the gallery followed by a perfect lunch. Sandra could tell her daughter was pre-occupied by something, but she didn't push it. She just enjoyed their time and was quite tired by the time they headed back to the house. "Thanks honey, but mama needs to put her feet up now." They both laughed as they kicked off their shoes and Noah brought them some sweet tea.

"Mother, we have some news we want to share with you. Before you go crazy, I am not pregnant or anything like that. And the wedding is still on." Noah chimed in, "this has more to do with a business opportunity." Sandra James was curious, and she asked Noah for a glass of wine before hearing what was coming. She had a feeling she needed something stronger than sweet tea for this story.

"We have a great opportunity to work closely with Senator Watkins in D.C. She wants us to move there so I can work in her D.C. office." "We have been talking it over for days and we decided to take Anastasia up on her offer!" "I know it is not going to be easy moving so much further north and we will miss everyone terribly. But we just must do this. We are really excited, and we want you to be happy for us. We will be moving in thirty days or sooner if we find a place to rent."

"Wow, I certainly wasn't expecting that news." Sandra was a bit in shock and not sure what to say but looking into her daughters' eyes she saw worry and excitement. Sandra James raised her daughter to not be afraid to try new things and to seek out adventure in life. So, this was one of those times. "I understand darlin' and I would love to visit you guys in D.C. when you are settled in." "How could I say working for a congressperson is a bad idea. It isn't. It is great!" "And I like that Watkins lady. She stands for good things, and I am proud she asked you to come to Washington. Just wow!"

"So, Noah, what are your plans for work?" "You have a great job here and I am sure you hate to leave it, right?"

"Well, it's funny the timing. I had been looking for something else that would challenge me more. I spoke to Anastasia, and she connected me with a local D.C. Art Institute Director, and I have a phone interview in a few days. I am excited to make a change and I can't let your daughter leave without me, soooo...."

They all laughed and talked for another hour about the big move and leaving friends, and everything else that comes with a big life change. The conversation had turned out better than expected. Abby was sure her mom would not want her to go so far away. She guessed it was time and she was happy her mom wanted to come visit. It was all going to be just fine.

Noah and Abby had also been talking over what to do with their Roswell home. Abby's mom suggested they keep it and rent it. "Then if you ever want to return to the area, you still own property here," said Sandra. Noah liked the idea so after some thinking about it, they decided to keep the Roswell house and rent it out. The friends thought that was a smart idea as well. In fact, Kendall and Chad had been considering moving in together and selling his condo. The couples began talking about the fact that Kendall should lease their Roswell home from them. "After all, you guys have a dog that would love a yard." Abby and Noah really would rather have their friends rent the house than lease it to strangers that would not take the best care of the place.

Kendall and Chad discussed it at length and decided it made sense to rent the house. They could bank the money they would make off both condos and maybe find something to invest their money in for the future. So, plans were set in place to make it happen.

Of course, Kendall had a ton of designer furniture and art pieces, so she met with a realtor friend who suggested she try to sell her condo furnished and just buy what they needed for the house. After all, a small craftsman bungalow would not look right filled with modern art and glass tables. And that eight-foot dining table needed to stay put. This was going to be a nice change. Kendall knew she had changed since meeting Chad. He owned a Harley Davidson motorcycle store, and he was a casual kind of guy. He had managed to rub off on Kendall over the last year and she found herself more interested in picnics in the park, hikes in the woods and lazy Sundays. Recently she was feeling tired of her modern, oversized condominium, and she needed a change. This move to Roswell would be good for her and Chad. They were excited about their life together.

As busy as the lady friends were with life plans and keeping up with politics, they were also busy planning the wedding of Noah and Abby. June was just around the corner, and it was time to go dress shopping. Abby insisted on touring some stores. She said the virtual dress shopping just was not for her. The friends agreed so plans were set in motion. Sandra James came back to town along with Noah's sister, Lilly. Noah and Abby had asked Lilly to be in the wedding. She lived in Denver, so it was a long trip back to Atlanta, but she was glad to be included. Lilly was Noah's only sibling, and they were very close. She was also very artistic, like her brother. In fact, she had moved to Denver a few years ago to open a jewelry store for her hand-made items. It was quite successful, and she was doing well, which made Noah very happy for his little sister. She had visited Noah and Abby over the holidays and Abby found her soon to be sister-in-law an interesting and fun person. They got along great and had kept in touch with facetime calls every couple of weeks.

Leona planned the dress shopping day. They had narrowed it down by shopping online and they only planned to visit one location that had three dresses Abby would choose from. After the decision was made, they would celebrate with lunch and champagne!

The team of five women met at the designer shop for the dress fittings. The store was modern and airy with lovely private rooms for each group. A personal attendant brought out the three dresses and swooped up Abby to go try on the first dress. It was a simple design with one shoulder strap and some beading along the sides. It was tight fitting and while Abby was slender, she did not like the fit and decided this was not the one. Her mother was glad because she did not think it suited her daughter in the least.

The next dress was so beautiful. Abby seemed to float out of the dressing room onto the pedestal in front of her friends. The dress was a cream color and a simple t on top with short sleeves made of lace. The bottom was slightly poufy with several layers of lace and a long train with a scalloped bottom. It fit Abby perfectly and her mother began to cry. "Oh, my goodness you are so beautiful darling", said Mrs. James. The girlfriends and her new sister-in-law to be all cheered and clapped and said, "you have to get that one!"

Abby smiled and she agreed. She had already ruled out the third dress in the dressing room. It was not the one. This dress felt perfect on her, and she loved it so much. "It must be the one, I guess." Abby felt a tear well up in her eye as she looked at her reflection in the oversized mirror. "I can't believe this is all real. I am really getting married to Noah James."

Just then the cork popped off the bottle of champagne that Leona had ordered from the shop. They all laughed and hugged Abby and the attendant snapped a photo of the group that was all smiles and tears.

The venue had already been decided upon over the Christmas holidays. Noah had spoken to the gallery owners about hosting a reception at the Art Gallery, to which they agreed immediately. They all loved Noah and hated to see him leaving them and this would be a wonderful sendoff they decided. Abby knew of a non-denominational small chapel in a city park not too far from the gallery location. It would work out perfectly to host the ceremony in the park chapel then make their way over to the gallery for the reception. Everything was booked and ready.

Anastasia had been going back and forth from Atlanta to Washington for two years now. She had kept an apartment in Atlanta and had bought a home in D.C. last year. She was Abby's boss, but also her friend and was thrilled to be her Maiden of Honor. She was not able to attend the dress purchase event but had been there for a wedding shower and other important planning events. In fact, she had been collaborating closely with the Art Gallery team to make the reception impressive and like no other wedding reception anyone had ever seen. She insisted on a live orchestra, ballroom dance floor area, and extravagant food and wine for a sit-down dinner of 100 people.

Anastasia worked out the guest list with Abby and Noah and the rest of the wedding team. She wanted this to be perfect and no expense was too much. Her wedding gift to the couple was to pay for the reception. Of course, the parents of the couple argued that fact but they lost out. Noah's parents even sent a check to Anastasia, and she promptly tore it up and insisted she would cover the cost.

It was now April, and the wedding was two months out, but work had not stopped at the congresswoman's office. And Noah had been accepted for a position in D.C. as the new Director of the Art Institute. The current Director had made a sudden decision to retire at the first of the year, so they were anxious for Noah to get to D.C. and start his job. Noah and Abby had already been to D.C. a couple of times looking at properties to lease. They were just waiting for some calls back.

Abby was sitting at her desk in Atlanta doing some work and got a call from a Washington area code. She answered with her usual "Hello, you have reached the office of Anastasia Watkins, how may I help you?" The response at the other end was "I am looking for Abigale James or Noah Armstrong please".

"This is Abigale, Abby, who is calling?"

"I am with the Withrow group, and you asked about leasing a townhouse here in D.C. near the capital.

You have been approved and the home is available May first." "We will need your deposit in three days and if you cannot occupy the home on May first, we will find a new tenant."

"Yes! We agree and of course we will be there! Oh my gosh, I am so excited to hear this. May I send you the deposit electronically please?"

"That will be fine. All paperwork is being emailed to you now. Please complete the final paperwork and return it with your deposit within 72 hours." "We look forward to having you here in D.C. soon. Thanks."

"Oh, thank you so much! I do have some questions so I will email you with those. Is that okay?"

"Yes ma'am. That is fine. Let me know if you need anything else." "The home has keyless entry and all information along with security codes will be in the email we sent to you today. Congratulations!" "Goodbye."

Reality is sinking in for Abby. They must move NOW! Before the wedding in June, they need to move and get settled into a new place with new jobs then return to Atlanta for their wedding. Suddenly the wedding plans seem to be flawed. Why didn't they wait, she thought. But there is no time to second guess anything today. She had to start making some calls. The first one is to Noah.

"Hi Honeybee!" "Remember how you said the other day that you wished we could just get a place in D.C. and get on with life?" "Well, we got a place, and it is that fantastic townhouse you loved so much on Champlain Street. They just called me, and it is ours on May first!"

"Wow, that is great! Wait a minute, May first?"

"Yes, I know, but we have to take it, right?"

"Of course, we do. I guess we sort of knew it would happen like this. No calls back for weeks then suddenly we must move today." "You know it is April 16th, right? That means we pack and move in two weeks babe." "Can we do that?"

"I guess we must if we want all this to work. I already told the realtor we would take it and the paperwork is in my email now. Can you get off early and meet me at Kendall's place? We need to finalize plans with her and Chad."

The good news is that Kendall and Chad both had contracts on their condo's, and they needed to be out by June so they can make this work. Abby made the rest of her phone calls to her mom, her friends and to her boss, Anastasia, who was thrilled to get Abby to D.C. asap.

Noah also had some calls to make to his family and his new boss in D.C. Then he asked his current boss for a quick meeting. They discussed his departure in two weeks and talked more about the wedding reception that would be taking place at the gallery. Noah was barely hearing a word as his mind was already on securing a moving company. He recalled that he had one on standby that just meant calling with a date and they were all set. His mind wandered and finally that meeting was over. As he was walking towards the door, his boss stopped him. "You know you have loads of unused vacation days Noah, I suggest you take a couple of weeks now and just get life in order. We have been planning for your leave and we are ready, so just get out of here. I will have your assistant pack up your office for you. We will ship everything to you. Just leave us your new address and we will take care of it. We will see you in June for the big day buddy!" The men had worked together for six years, and they hugged, which was unusual, even for them. Noah decided to take him up on the offer and he texted Abby that he would see her at Kendall's tonight.

CHAPTER EIGHT

Leona Branson had been working diligently in Atlanta as a Consultant and Marketing Director for Congresswoman Watkins. They had put together hundreds of meetings with the *Gray-Haired* groups throughout the country. Leona loved politics and watching as things began to change. The news media could not even explain the uncertainty of what was happening. Suddenly, women everywhere were finding their voices again. The tides had turned in the last two years and a focus was on the new congresswoman, Anastasia Watkins. There was no getting around it. She was leading the charge for women's rights, environmental protection agencies, technology, and mostly social changes across the country. There was even a whisper of her running for

President in the next term.   So, Leona was more than just a little busy keeping ahead of news stories about her boss and planning secret meetings with the various powerhouses in the women's movements across the nation. A few walk-ins took place in Washington and leaders in business all wanted a meeting with Mrs. Watkins. She was very popular these days. Leona found herself visiting D.C. a couple of times this month and she enjoyed the travel and being inside in Washington. Not everyone knew things that she knew. And on her last trip to meet with Anastasia, along with helping her friends Noah and Abby get moved into their townhouse, she met a certain businessman by the name of Tucker Jackson. He had been persistent in his attempts to secure a meeting with her boss to discuss changes to the abortion laws. Since this was a continuous hot topic for Anastasia, she finally met with Tucker for dinner and had Leona join them.

Once the business was out of the way, Tucker and Leona talked over desert and wine for another hour or more. Anastasia left them as she could see the sparks flying and wanted to give her friend a chance to explore this handsome man without her boss at the table.

Leona was smitten at once by Tucker. She heard about his life in California, prior to moving to

D.C. for work. He had been a lobbyist for a female doctor in Los Angeles and he ended up working for a medical consulting company in D.C. They put together abortion and medical rights business strategies for physicians and regularly meet with politicians to pave the way for changes in laws to protect women. All this was very much related to the causes being rallied by Leona's boss and most of what they both believed in lined up perfectly. Also, Tucker just happened to be 38 years old and unmarried and had the face and body of a model. He was almost too much for Leona. She had quizzed him extensively about life and love and he was really a regular guy that had no idea just how handsome he was. She found that cute.

Tucker found Leona captivating as well and following that dinner they spent hours emailing and texting and making late night calls back and forth. Leona found herself wanting to tell Tucker about her amazing boss and the secret society they had created, but she knew she could not. In fact, all her friends had agreed to a secret oath, and they could tell no husband, fiancé, or boyfriend any details. She was fairly certain that each of them kept their word.

Late one evening the phone rang at Leona's home. "Hello", it was her new man. "How was your day?"

"Oh, it was okay. I couldn't stop thinking about this long-legged lady I met a couple of weeks ago. For some reason I cannot get her out of my mind."

Leona smiled on the end of the line. She felt like a schoolgirl with a crush. It had been a long time since she had these kinds of feelings. "Well, I am sorry you are having such trouble with your thoughts. Maybe you should come by here for dinner and explain all this in more detail." She laughed out loud. Tucker laughed back. "Sounds good to me. What time shall I arrive?" "Oh, let's say 6:30ish." "See you then pretty lady."

It was June now and the wedding of Noah and Abby would take place soon. Everyone was busy making all the last-minute plans. Noah and Abby had settled into their new townhome in D.C. and Noah was extremely busy getting the lay of the land in his new job. They were so grateful for the wonderful family and friends that kept the ship afloat for them. Anastasia had been making a lot of calls to be sure everything was in place. She took time with Abby to steady her nerves and they had become close friends. The two of them were almost inseparable in recent weeks. Anastasia's husband Hank was busy with his own investment company, so he was glad his wife had such a close friend when he was away traveling. He didn't like leaving Anastasia alone. There were too many crazies out there and Hank often reminded her of it.

Hank was away on a weeklong business trip. He knew Anastasia and Abby had some last-minute wedding stuff to discuss and Abby planned to stay the weekend before the wedding at Anastasia's place. Noah was on board, and he understood.

Anastasia made her goodnight phone call to Hank, and he told her to enjoy her "girl time" with her friend. She got busy putting together some snacks and selected a bottle of nice French red wine to share with Abby. She so looked forward to this down time. And she was truly excited for her friend and the upcoming wedding.

Anastasia heard her doorbell ring, and she was sure it was Abby. It was Friday night around seven and Abby had said she couldn't be there until nine but maybe something had changed. Anastasia trotted to the door ready for her girl's weekend and opened the door. Before she could slam it shut, the giant man wearing a black ski mask, shoved her to the ground and immediately pounded her over the back of the head with something. It knocked her out completely.

Anastasia came back to consciousness and looked around in her dazed half-awakened mind. She realized she was tied to a dining room chair. Her feet were tied tight, and her hands tied behind her back. Was it rope or something else? She wasn't sure. She was suddenly very aware of what was happening. Her head ached terribly. Her neck hurts. She saw blood on the carpet and realized it was running down her neck, onto her shirt, then dripping onto the floor beneath her chair. "What do you want?" "Who are you?" Her screams went unanswered, and the man was not there. Then she heard him. He was talking to someone. She wasn't sure if they were also in her house or if he was on the phone. She tried to listen and could hear a few words. "I have her…. tied up…out of it now…." Then she heard him say "she will pay for her sins, stupid woman", and she blacked out again.

Anastasia awoke for a second time. She looked at the clock on the wall and it was now eight o'clock. She has been out for a while. The blood had stopped dripping from her body but the large circle on the floor told her she had lost a lot of blood. She was wondering what this man wanted, and where was her friend, and what could she do to escape this torture? Think.

Suddenly the man in the mask appeared before her. He was rambling on about women and how he had to stop her and her friends from taking over the world and killing all the men and taking all the jobs. His rambling sounded crazy. And she saw he was holding a hammer in one hand and a gun in the other. Anastasia began to shake all over. She was always so in control and so brave, and now she feels scared to death, tied up, no control over any of this. What does he plan to do to her? Kill her? Who is he talking with on the phone. She tries to make sense of it, but nothing makes sense. Her head is pounding.

"Hey, where are you? Do you want money?" "I can help you if you let me." "Please, take whatever you want and go." "For God's sake man, tell me what you want!" Now she was getting mad. This is ridiculous. My friend will be here soon and then what? Crap, I must warn Abby, but how, she thought.

The man was back and was waving the hammer around. He pointed the gun at Anastasia and said he would shoot her if she tried to escape. "Where would I go? I am tied up." Then she muttered in a low voice, "you moron." The man heard her. He screamed loudly, "so you think I am stupid, huh?" "Who is the one tied to the chair; you be the stupid one." Then he mumbled again and ran from the room to the kitchen.

Abby was a little early, but she knew her friend was expecting her. She pulled into the drive and saw a strange truck parked there that she had never seen before. It was an older model ford truck with no license plates. Abby thought that was strange. She texted her friend to say she was here. Inside, Anastasia's phone binged. It was in the pocket of her robe. But she could not get her hands loose. She hoped the man in the kitchen did not hear it. It seemed not, since he did not come back. All Anastasia could think of was what was next and how to warn her friend. She mumbled in her brain, "please do not knock on my door, walk away, get out of here." I have to warn her before he kills us both, she thought.

Abby walked up to the house and the dining room was lit. The rest of the house was dark. It caused Abby to stare into the house and she could see her friend. She could see the blood on her face and that she was tied. Just then the masked man came into the room and Abby dove into the bushes by the front door. She could not believe what she was seeing. She was holding her phone, and she began to dial 9-1-1. "Help me. My friend, congresswoman Watkins home on 5th street, hurry. A man is in her home now…. I, I think she is tied up and she is hurt. I am outside. Please hurry, now, please."

The man thought he heard something outside and went to open the front door. Anastasia yelled out. "Help!" The man ran back to her and began waving the gun in her face. Anastasia asked again, "what do you want from me?"

"I want you to shut the hell up. You stupid woman and all your stupid ideas. You got my wife and her friends all worked up about getting jobs and getting paid more money. Women need to stay home and cook. They need to know the place for them." Then they both heard it. Sirens. Yes, Anastasia thought, someone knows what is happening in here. The man looked confused. He said, "what did you do stupid woman?" "You gonna pay for this." He began to raise the hammer and his hostage screamed as loud as she could scream and managed to knock over the chair with her body tied to it. She fell into the puddle of blood on the carpet and continued to yell out for help. Abby rammed herself against the front door and it banged open, just as the police car came rushing through the yard. Abby yelled out and ran to her friend and the masked man ran past her towards the front door. The police ran squarely into the intruder and the gun went off. The man was wrestled to the ground by three officers and there was no escape for him. The intruder was quickly put into handcuffs and dragged away.

Abby ran to her friends' side and began to untie the knotted ropes. There was so much blood everywhere. She managed to untie Anastasia's feet and then pulled the chair upright. Anastasia was crying and shaking as her friend untied her hands and grabbed her limp body and pulled her close to her. "You are okay, I have you now."

Just then the ambulance arrived and the EMT's attended to Anastasia. The police had called for backup and at least five more squad cars had arrived on the scene. They spoke to Abby about what happened. Anastasia was taken to the hospital for treatment and Abby asked one of the officers if he could take her to the hospital to stay with her friend, which he agreed to do. On the car ride Abby called Noah and he met her at the hospital. Once the doctor gave them an update and told them Anastasia had a concussion but would recover, they decided to call Hank and give him the news.

Noah insisted the nurse check Abby over too and make sure she was okay to go home. She explained how she was "just fine" and just "shaken up a bit", but they looked her over just the same. Noah nearly cried when Abby explained all that had happened tonight. "What if you would have been there already?" "This could have been you laying in that bed." He was beside himself and Abby assured him she was fine.

Before the couple could make calls to family and friends and explain the news, the media had picked up the story and it was all over the television and internet. "Masked intruder attacked congresswoman Watkins with a gun and a hammer." "Watkins and her assistant held hostage." Abby had to explain to everyone that she just showed up in time to call the police. Hank flew home at once to be by his wife's side at the hospital.

Anastasia was released two days later. The doctors wanted her to stay a few more days but she insisted on being released. She had a wedding to attend at the end of the week. Doctors recommended that she not travel but she ignored them. There was no way she was missing this wedding. Abby and Noah discussed postponing things, but that would not be possible. After several conversations with Anastasia and Hank, who agreed to drive to Georgia in lieu of flying, the wedding was a go.

The media had a field day with this story. It turned out that the attacker was working alone. He had been on the phone with his estranged wife and was telling her how he had to stop this woman from changing the world with her power. The wife had left months earlier when her husband was acting crazy and had bought a gun. She told everything to the police and the masked man would pay for this crime.

Behind the scenes, the secret society created by Anastasia and her team was thriving. They had come together and agreed they would continue on their path. The world needed them now more than ever. Anastasia was escorted to the wedding by her husband and a few close friends. Extra security was set up to watch the travel brigade and extra security was at the wedding chapel and the reception. Reporters were now following Anastasia everywhere and this included the wedding. Abby and Noah understood, and they were just happy their friend was doing well.

Hank stayed close to his wife that week and insisted on her not going to her office. She was fine with that and while she insisted, she was doing fine, it was nice to be out of the public eye for a few days, and to cuddle at home with Hank and get some needed rest. They spent hours talking about their life together and how much time they spent apart for work. The two agreed to make some changes and do better in the future. They would not travel as much, and they would beef up security around Anastasia since she planned to stay in the public arena.

The motor brigade made the day trip to Atlanta on Friday and there was a quiet rehearsal dinner with the group of friends in the evening. Everyone was thrilled to see Anastasia looking so well. She said her makeup lady was a rock star! She managed to cover her bumps and bruises and she was more than ready for the big event.

The wedding went off without a hitch. Only forty close family members and friends attended the ceremony. The Art Gallery hosted 100 people inside and many onlookers were outside the venue trying to get a look at the wedding couple and a peek at the congresswoman. Security was tight and they had no issues at all.

Abby wore her cream-colored flowing gown and carried a small bouquet of yellow roses. Anastasia, Leona and Kendall along with Lilly all wore light yellow dresses. The gentlemen wore cream jackets and brown slacks. The reception was like something from a movie set. One reporter was allowed inside for a few photos before guests arrived. She wrote that the place was stunning with beautiful artwork, ice sculptures and flowers in abundance. One glass artist created a hanging glass display with various colors of yellow, gold and blue. A water feature against one wall was nine feet tall and six feet wide and blue water poured over urns and rocks, splashing into a small pool below. A small orchestra was placed in an upstairs loft and music seemed to fall over the railings and down the stairs into the flower filled room. Tables for six lined the walls and there was a dance floor created from colored acrylic squares that lit up when you stepped on it. Each table centerpiece was a two-foot-tall bouquet in a gold vase and the chairs were gold with yellow flowers tied to the back. Each guest had a small box with a special thank you gift inside. Nobody would say what the box held.

Anastasia had worked diligently with her makeup crew to be sure her facial cuts and bruises were concealed. She laughed when she realized during the ceremony that all the ladies now had grey hair. Some were natural and some were not. But they each wore their hair grey, some long and some short, and they were all beautiful. Anastasia was lucky to have this group of friends. My beautiful gray-haired friends, she thought.

There was one unexpected guest. Tucker Jackson had been invited by Anastasia. She was still trying to play matchmaker with him and Leona. Anastasia was certain they made a good pair. Tucker was reluctant at first, but Anastasia was persistent and even offered him some part time work for her office if he would just travel with her and Hank to Atlanta. Not wanting to let the congresswoman down, Tucker agreed to make the trip. He would travel with the Watkins in their limo from DC to Atlanta. This would give him plenty of facetime with Anastasia.

Abby and Noah enjoyed the evening. It all went as planned. During a late evening dance Abby whispered in the ear of her beloved, "How is it that I found you and made you mine? I am the luckiest girl in the world. I love you honeybee."

Noah replied with a smile and spun her around in her perfectly splendid wedding gown. He mouthed the words "I love you more" as he twirled his sweetheart. The party was everything and more.

At the reception Anastasia quickly introduced Tucker to Leona. "Darling Leona, you remember Tucker Jackson, don't you dear?" Leona played along knowing well that she had spent several evenings of late with this fine gentleman.

"Oh, of course I do. It is good to see you again Tucker. It has been a while. Do you know my friends Noah and Abby?"

Tucker stumbled a bit trying to explain why he was in attendance. Anastasia jumped in to rescue him and explained how he was such a close friend to her and Hank that they asked him to make the trip with them so they could visit on the long drive here. She also wanted to introduce Tucker to everyone because she was hoping to have him do some work for her.

Leona bought it and was happy to see this handsome man again. They ended up sitting together for most of the evening and talking for hours. Finally, Tucker asked for a dance and Leona felt an immediate warmth running down her spine. Every time their bodies touched there was an unexplainable spark between the two. Leona did not object to the feelings.

The friends partied until late at night and then said their goodbyes. Noah and Abby were off to honeymoon in France for two weeks. All the girls were jealous and happy for their friends. They deserved this and more. They are good people, thought each one of their friends. Tonight was a good night! The ordeal with Anastasia had given them a good fright, but this just made the group of them more determined than ever to succeed. The toasts were especially warm-hearted and filled with loving statements from close friends and family. It was a night to remember for sure!

Tucker enjoyed himself as well and he could not get enough time with Leona. He guessed his friends were correct in their assumption that the two of them would hit it off if given the opportunity. Tucker found Leona to be smart and funny and he loved her smile. She had a way about herself that was soft and assuring. He hung on to her every word. He offered to take her for a drink at the end of the reception, but Leona was just too tired tonight. She explained how she had to get some rest and loved the evening and she hoped they could pick up soon in DC. Leona was thinking she should play it safe and not jump in too quickly with this handsome man. He happened to be the most eligible bachelor in DC according to the tabloids. Leona needed some time to think after a long night of partying. Tucker agreed to call it a night.

CHAPTER NINE

The wedding was a success and Anastasia was glad to be headed back to D.C. soon. But she had planned to visit some family and stop in at the Atlanta office to see her staff there. She was not looking her best yet and was using extra face cream and makeup to cover her battle wounds from the home invasion. Hank had been worried sick over her and refused to leave her side. While they were in Atlanta, they were having extra security alarms installed around the D.C. property. They had given statements to the police, and it was clear the intruder acted alone. But the internet would not let the story fade and the group of women that supported their Senator was doing everything in their power to protect her. The *Secret Society of Grey-Haired Women* had grown to include thousands of women around the United States. They had managed to stay as underground as possible, but more and more leaks had come out recently about some type of women's group supporting political changes. Several reporters were on the case and doing their best investigating to figure it out. So far, all good, according to Leona and Kendall.

The two ladies met Anastasia in private at the Atlanta office. They talked about the wedding and other personal relationship stuff then got into the business end of things. Hank was sent off on a golf date with Chad and Tucker. The women went over several new bills introduced and voted into law. It had been a very successful couple of years. Anastasia had a huge following and now she gained more who were sympathetic to her recent trauma and how tough she was in handling it and getting on with business. Leona knew the police ruled out anyone else involved but she found quite a bit of dark web traffic about the home invasion and too many characters making comments about how Anastasia "deserved it" and that she "got what was coming to her", so Leona wanted her boss to be extra careful when she was back in D.C.

Kendall also agreed that there was a creepy vibe to this guy, and he didn't seem smart enough to have acted alone. She told her boss they needed to keep looking deeper into the incident and do their own investigation.

"Anastasia, you are a powerful person, and you have a ton of good followers, but there are just as many people trying to destroy the work you have done." Leona had to speak up while she was face-to-face with her boss.

"I know dear. I am not a fool. And I know you mean well. I just don't want this guy or anyone else to think he got to me, so to speak." "With your ladies help I have been able to move mountains in Congress. I can see the tide turning for us. We even have a new freedom bill that should be going through this week. It allows businesses to cover day care costs for their employees and get some of the cost back from the federal government. We have been funding the program and it is finally taking off!" "They are not going to stop us now."

"This is fantastic!", said Kendall. "We are pretty impressive aren't we." "I am so proud to be doing this work with you and Leona and Abby."

Just then, someone came rushing through the office door where the women were meeting. "I tried to stop him", said the office administrator Joey. "He just wouldn't take no for an answer, ma'am."

"It's okay Joey. I got this."

"Can I help you sir?" Leona and Kendall had jumped out of their chairs. Everyone was a bit on edge after Anastasia's attack last week. It was too soon for someone to just break down the door to her office.

"My God Man – is the building on fire?" Leona was ready to punch him in the face.

"Sorry ladies, but I just had to speak with the Senator before she left town. My boss insisted I get a statement from you Ms. Watkins." "Can you give me some kind of statement about the home invasion and if you are really, okay?" "I mean, you look fine, but…"

"For goodness sakes young man. Who are you and who do you work for, for starters?" Said Anastasia.

"I am Dan Pennington, a reporter with the Times."

"A lot of people want to hear from you since it has been over a week and you just up and left town."

"Well, I am in Atlanta to try to meet with my staff, but that is proving difficult. And I attended a friend's wedding as well. Kendall here will give you a more detailed statement explaining that I am indeed just fine." "Now I must get back to my hotel and pack for my trip home. I will talk to you ladies later."

Kendall and Leona were giving Mr. Pennington the evil eye for interrupting their meeting with the boss. Kendall did as instructed and provided a bit more information to the reporter so he would leave them alone. She decided this may be a good opportunity to pick up more followers, so she asked the reporter to meet her for a drink at 5:00 pm in the hotel lobby.

Kendall called her boss/friend and gave Anastasia a heads up about her plan. Kendall knew there was a convention in town of women CEOs. They were meeting at the hotel to discuss several new business ventures in technology, AI and of all things, space travel. One of the companies was building a new type of space station and the woman CEO was getting lots of press.

Kendall had a plan for the top three CEOs to ask for a photo with Anastasia as she was leaving the hotel this afternoon. Pennington would get all the photos and the big story for *The New York Times*!

Kendall and Leona both filled in Hank and Anastasia, and they had a plan. They explained to Pennington he should bring his camera for a few pictures of the Senator. And just as planned, Anastasia arrived in the hotel lobby at 5:15, she shook hands with and chatted with the CEO group, and Pennington snapped away with his camera!   The group of women was thrilled to see their Senator friend and obliged for photos.

Tucker Jackson was there, and he drew some attention as well. Tucker was known in DC for his prior lobbyist work in California. He was also a big shot businessman, and he loved politics! The reporter recognized him right away.

"Excuse me, Mr. Jackson, are you traveling with the Senator? Are you here on business Sir?"

Tucker responded that he was also attending a wedding and he left it at that. He did smile for the camera and did his share of shaking hands with the CEOs in the lobby. He was a politician at heart.

Anastasia and Hank said their goodbyes and headed to their limousine. Pennington got his big story, and everything seemed to be getting back to normal, for now at least. Anastasia decided that while her assistant was on her honeymoon, she too would just take a little time off. After all, the last ten days had shaken her to the core. She would never let anyone know this. But Anastasia was just barely keeping it together since the assault. Hank was very aware though and he had pushed her to take a little time off. The pair had secretly booked a private estate in the Greek Islands, with extra security, and they told nobody, except Kendall, where they would be.

Kendall explained to Leona the plan. She said she could not say exactly where their boss was going but that she would be checking in daily with her. Leona understood. The wedding and all the planning had been a lot, and both ladies agreed they all could use some down time. They wrapped up for the night and decided they would both take a personal day tomorrow.

"See you Wednesday back in DC my friend!"

"And don't call me!" "Get some rest."

"Bye!"

Tucker made one last move with Leona. She saw him walking her way and smiled. He was so easy on her eyes, and she suddenly had that warm feeling again.

"Hi there handsome."

"Hi yourself pretty lady. Are you headed to the airport as well?"

"I leave tomorrow. Just wrapping up some things tonight. It was nice having you join us for the reception last night. I had a good time."

Tucker quickly grabbed Hank's arm and told him he would not be riding back to DC with him and Anastasia. He would get a flight home tomorrow. He thanked them for the invitation, and he would call Anastasia when they returned from Greece.

"Sorry about that Leona. Had to let Hank know not to wait for me. I am flying home tomorrow as well. So, I guess I will need someone to have dinner with me tonight."

"Hmm, I sure wish I knew someone. I guess if you are really desperate, I could join you."

"Consider me desperate then. How about we meet in the lobby at six?"

"That sounds perfect. I can wrap up my work and get refreshed for dinner. I will see you in a bit."

Leona was beside herself. She felt like a 38-year-old teenager. She quickly texted her friends to let them know she was having dinner with Tucker tonight. Kendall responded right away with a thumbs up and said, "go for it girl".

Tucker was prompt and met Leona in the lobby at 5:59. He had changed into a nice suit jacket and slacks and was wearing very nice shoes. This impressed Leona. She had gone quickly to the hotel shops and bought a new dress for the evening. It was black and form fitting, showing off her nice fit form. She wore strappy heels that accentuated her muscular legs gained from her daily workouts. It was "now or never" she thought. So much for being careful and taking her time.

"Well, now. Don't you clean up nicely. Love the dress. How is it you are not taken yet?" Tucker smiled as he said this.

Leona smiled back. "I don't understand it myself. I guess my Mr. Wonderful has not appeared just yet. But I am still looking."

The pair left the hotel arm-in-arm and grabbed a car to head out for dinner. They had the auto-driver drop them a few blocks away in a nice Buckhead restaurant that was popular with the who's who of Atlanta. Leona had been here a few times in the past, but not in recent years. It was nice to be in a familiar setting.

"Oh, I love this place. What a great choice. And they have the best wine as well."

Dinner lingered for a couple of hours. Everything was wonderful and conversation was light. Then Tucker began to talk politics. He adored Anastasia. He had known her and Hank for many years. He was a big supporter of her, and they agreed on many platforms. In fact, Anastasia had been trying to get Tucker to run for office for the last few years. First, she wanted him to run for Governor of California several years ago, and then she tried to convince him to go for an open Senate seat two years ago. But Tucker explained how his business was taking off and he had moved his headquarters to DC just last year. He had been working with Anastasia behind the scenes on some abortion rights laws and worked with many physicians across the country to help change the laws that tied their hands.

Leona found it all interesting. She wondered why Anastasia kept her friend a secret. Tucker seemed to want it that way. He didn't want to be in the spotlight. But it seemed he was headed in that direction now that Anastasia asked him to come work with her on her possible new campaign.

"Yes, she told me a couple of weeks ago about her thoughts of running for office. I do need to tell you something else. I think I can do that now. Anastasia asked me to consider being her running mate, if and when it happens. I am still thinking about all of that.

"Vice President?" "Oh my gosh! That is fantastic Tucker. What an honor."

"I know, right. She has been grooming me for a couple of years now. I am just not sure. I think she has a higher opinion of my skills set than I do."

"Well, she is a smart lady, and she would never ask you to do this if she was not one hundred percent certain it was the right choice."

Leona then began to wonder again why Anastasia would not have talked about this with her team before just making Tucker this offer. She had questions running through her head now but decided to concentrate on her date for now. She was enjoying herself immensely. But now there is added pressure. This man sitting next to her could potentially be the next Vice President of the United States one day.

"Could I get another glass of wine please? I think I am going to need it."

After dinner the duo moved to the bar area for a bit more conversation and a brandy before heading back to the hotel. They talked for another hour and the conversation was easy. They both enjoyed exercise and morning runs. He was a cat person which Cher would love to hear. They liked jazz and walks in the park and their favorite holiday was Christmas. Tucker was forty on his birthday this year. He had been in a long-term relationship that ended when he found out she was cheating on him during his travels out of town. He had been quite cautious since then and did not date much.

At the hotel Tucker said he really wanted to ask Leona back to his room, but he understood it was just too soon for that. Leona was a little disappointed, but she agreed they needed more time to get to know one another better. There was time for that in DC she thought. They kissed goodnight in the elevator and neither of them wanted the night to end. Tucker said goodnight and stepped off the elevator to his floor.

Just as the door was closing Leona put her hand in the door. "Wait. I just cannot let the night end yet. Can I please get one more kiss from you Mr. Wonderful?"

Tucker grabbed her close and the doors closed behind them. He put his arm around her and walked her down the hallway and opened his hotel room door.

"Please come in dear. I would love to give you that kiss you requested."

With that smile and a wink Tucker pulled her close and they kissed as the heat built up in intensity between them. They could not stop. They both did not want to stop. Suddenly they were staring into each other's eyes as their bodies pressed tightly together. There was no music playing but the two of them felt music like soft jazz circling around them. They moved as one, body and soul, making love for hours, until they could no longer move. They were spent. Their bodies were limp and satisfied and their hearts both pounded, and their eyes met again. Nothing was said, but they both understood what the other was feeling. It was warm and lovely, and they wanted the night to last forever.

Tucker held his new love closely and asked her if the kiss was good. She smiled and confirmed that it was perfect. It was now 4:00 a.m. They both laughed when they realized they were not going to make an early morning flight back to DC. They would get there eventually. For now, they would sleep.

CHAPTER TEN

Leona sat up in bed. Life has been a whirlwind since she started dating Tucker. They have had such fun this last year. And he has been doing more work with Anastasia. The friends have all accepted the new couple as a permanent thing. But now there are other things to concentrate on. She must start working on the baby shower for Abby and Noah. It is hard to imagine her best friends as parents. They would be fine. They just need to work a bit less. They are both so busy but determined to have a family before Abby turns forty.

Leona calls Kendall to chat. "Hi girl. What is on your calendar today? Are you all doing anything on this Sunday?"

"No ma'am. It is a down day. Do we need to work on the baby shower?"

"Yes, please help me. I am stuck. Not sure where to start. Can we get some lunch and come up with some ideas?"

"Okay, sounds good. Text me where and when and I can be there. I think Chad has plans anyway."

Leona and Kendall meet at their favorite spot in DC for lunch. The group of friends now all live in the DC area. It was only a matter of time with all the ladies working for the congresswoman. They have not only survived, but they have thrived in Washington this last year. Kendall's mom visits monthly, and Noah's parents seem to find a reason to visit every few weeks. It will be more often when that grandbaby arrives, thought Leona.

Kendall had several fun ideas, and the friends came up with a plan. Abby wanted to include Noah so it would be a couple's party. Details were ironed out before they shared all the plans with Abby. Anastasia wanted to host at her lavish home that had a wonderful garden. They would keep it to just about 10 couples and the parents of Noah and Abby.

Abby signed off on the plan. The baby girl was due in October so the event would happen in August. It was just July 1st so there was plenty of time to make plans and get the out-of-town guests some travel arrangements. Travel these days was crazy and flights were twice as costly as they were a few years ago. You could enter a lottery for reduced prices, but most folks had no time or energy for that process.

The Gray-Haired-Ladies had been hard at work for several years now. Recently there was a lot of reporting about who was doing what in politics. Anastasia was on the watch list for the next Presidential election. Her name was being tossed around and she was invited to every notable event in DC. She had visited with the current President on a couple of occasions recently and she had shared a lot of information with her groups. Some things she was unable to discuss of course.

Anastasia called a meeting with her DC team. She invited Tucker to attend the meeting as well. Her tough team of ladies listened as she laid out plans for their future. She decided it would include a bid for the Presidency. But if she wanted to be on the ticket next year, she had to declare herself now. There were new rules surrounding the presidential race since the two-party system no longer existed. A person that was qualified and wanted to run had to state so at least one year prior to the election. Then, at least five public officials had to confirm their acceptance of the potential candidate. Once that was completed the plans could go forward. The potential candidates then could only begin actual campaigning publicly three months prior to the election. Gone were the days of year-long campaign speeches. Most of the public embraced the new rules.

There was a big event coming up in October and Anastasia was the keynote speaker. The host was an environmental group that was gaining ground with the White House and the attention of the public and business leaders around the world. Anastasia decided this would be her time to throw her hat in the ring!

After a couple of hours of discussion, the group agreed they were behind her. Abby, however, was not able to head up the campaign since she was about to give birth. Kendall and Leona agreed to chair the campaign together. Of course, Abby insisted on collaborating with them behind the scenes as much as possible.

Kendall was certain she knew why Tucker was in attendance. But she waited for Anastasia to tell the group. "I do want to add one thing to what we have talked about today. It is very important. A President needs a good Vice President and I have chosen my running mate. Tucker Jackson has agreed to join me on this journey. People, I give you my Vice President nominee, Tucker Jackson!"

The group cheered and clapped, and Tucker was all smiles, as usual. He made a short speech and thanked his running mate and the group.

After the meeting the friends made their way to the local bar across the street from the office. Tucker stayed behind to talk with Anastasia. He told Leona he would catch up with her later. This group of co-workers and friends had become regulars here. The place was usually full of the regular suspects from Capitol Hill, but it was not too crowded tonight. The room was dimly lit and filled with dark leather chairs and stools, and it had an old-world vibe that appealed to the friends. Noah arrived and just behind him was Chad with a friend in tow. The ladies wanted to discuss what had just happened with Anastasia, but not with this stranger at the table. Leona leaned over to Kendall and whispered in her ear, "what was Chad thinking? Who is this guy?"

"This is his best buddy these days. All I hear about is Mark, Mark, Mark. I guess he has a Harley or something. Chad has been wanting us to meet him."

"So, Mark. My name is Abby, and this is my husband, Noah. We are all friends here. Glad to meet you."

"Hi, I am Leona. I must approve all of Chad's friends so we will talk more later." The group laughed and they all shook hands and exchanged smiles.

Leona had to admit this Mark guy was cute in a boyish way. He had a baby face, she thought. But under that jacket it looked like some fierce pecks. Her mind was wandering when Chad broke her spell. "Mark is a stand-up guy. He is originally from the Atlanta area, and I met him at my Harley shop years ago. He came into our store last month, and we hit it off right away."

Noah ordered drinks for the group and juice for Abby. They decided to put conversations about work on hold for the evening and get to know their new friend. After a few rounds of darts, the friends split up and headed home for the night. Mark asked Leona if she would stay for a nightcap with him, but she told him she had to get home. She was in a committed relationship with Tucker now, so she no longer looked at other men.

Mark was doing a fine job of wooing Leona, but she managed to keep her guard up. This guy was just a bit too friendly, too fast, and there was something about him that Leona found unsettling. She could not put her finger on it, but he was too nice, too cute, and too interested in her work and her friends. The guy had a lot of questions in between beers and darts. He seemed really interested in Leona's boss. A bit too interested in Leona's mind, so she shut him down and called it a night. Mark was a perfect gentleman and gave Leona his business card and said to call him sometime.

In the auto-drive home Leona looked at the card. Mark Hunter, Realtor – Washington, DC. Owner/Agent. The photo appeared to be recent. At the bar Mark had said he brokered his own business, and he had a side hustle selling antiques. He supposedly had a small antique shop just outside of DC and invited Leona to stop by sometime if she was in the area. He had scribbled an address on a bar napkin and put it in her pocket as she hopped into her car to leave. Leona just remembered this and felt in her pocket for the napkin. She pulled it out and looked at it. She made note of the address and crumpled the napkin and discarded it on the car seat before exiting the vehicle.

Leona called Kendall and gave her the lowdown on the evening. Kendall thought Mark was nice looking and very nice. "He did seem to have a lot of interest in our boss though. I thought that a bit strange too." The ladies agreed they would call it a night and they would have a lot to discuss tomorrow with the boss now about to launch a presidential campaign!

Chad asked Kendall what she thought about his new buddy. "Oh, he was nice enough. He had a lot of questions about Anastasia, and I guess he asked Leona a lot of questions after we left, so she is cautious."

"Oh really?"

"He did say he had some kind of antique shop, and he thought your boss was a collector or something."

"Chad, guess what Anastasia told us today…. She is going to go for it. You know. The White House!"

"What? She said that today? Wow, that is amazing! Why didn't you say something earlier?"

"Well, you showed up with Mark so we really couldn't say anything. It is not official yet. You can't say anything you know."

"I know the drill. How long have we been together now? Not to worry. That is damn good news honey. I am glad she is going for it. She is formidable for sure."

"Well, you know what this is going to mean for me right? I will be working on her campaign around the clock for the next year. Are you okay with that?"

"What if I was not okay? Would it matter? I am kidding you. I knew when I up and moved to DC a year ago that I would be in for a wild ride with you and your friends. I love you babe. You just do you!"

"Chadwick, I love you too. You are my rock. I could not do any of this without you in my corner. I hope you know how important you are to me honey."

"Come here sexy and show me how important I am. And then I will show you how important you are to me. Okie Dokey!" Chad grabbed Kendall and hugged her tight and began to undress her. She was so hot to him right now. He had to have her. All of her. This powerhouse of a woman, his friend, his partner, his life.

The morning brought all kinds of crazy. Headlines in the news were of the Governor of California putting his name in the hat for a Presidential nomination. The media was all over this. Wesly Camden was loved by some and hated by others in the political arena. There was no middle of the road for this guy. You either loved him or hated him. He was so outspoken about everything. No topic was off limits. He had a big toothy smile, blonde beachboy locks and a west coast tan. He dressed like a movie star and had done some Hollywood acting several years before hitting the campaign trail.

The Watkins team all arrived early to the office hoping to beat the boss there. No such luck. Anastasia had heard the news at 5 a.m. so she was up and running early. It was 7:15 and everyone was there.

"Well good morning chickadees. What a great day to be alive in Washington. Does anyone else feel like kicking some butts today?" The room was alive now and buzzing with chatter. Anastasia continued to address her team. "Well, I am not surprised by the news. Wesly is just going to have to learn the hard way that his old school politics won't work here in DC. Times have changed ladies and gentlemen. There is going to be a campaign like none in history and I am thrilled to be heading up this tsunami! Who is with me?"

The crowd of a dozen mostly women roared. "Go get 'em Anastasia!" "We are with you sister!" "It is time for the women of America to rise up and take their spot in history." Abby, Leona and the rest were shaking their fists now. There was an energy in the room. They all looked at one another and they knew it was going to happen. And they were all going to be a part of it. It was pure adrenaline and excitement. They were all ready.

The day was filled with meetings. Calendars were synchronized and dates plotted out for announcements. Anastasia put out a private message to her underground group of Gray-Haired-Ladies. It was more of a demand than a request.

Attention: Secret Society of Gray-Haired Women

Be on the call Tuesday, September 10th, 2052, at 10:30 a.m. eastern time. Private code: awpres54.

It was all hands on deck. Abby sat with her boss and friend for hours going over a speech. They managed to cover a lot and Anastasia was prepared for the call of her life tomorrow. Her usual way of doing things was to ad-lib a lot and not use too many prepared speeches. But this time it was different. She had to get this right and she wanted to cover a lot so there were few questions at the end. They estimated that approximately 3,000 women would be on this call from all over the world. Mostly calls would come from within the US but some members were traveling in other countries but needed to be on the call. Once the word was out about the call the phones began to ring. The set response was "please be on the call" and nothing more.

Tuesday was intense for everyone. Once this call went out there was no turning back. And the secret society would likely be secret no more. The members that supported Anastasia understood the code. But once the campaigning begins, the supporters will be out there in the public circles, and it will suddenly be an awakening of sorts for those that had no idea this lady had such a vast following. It would be a wave of powerful women coming to the forefront and waving their flag for this candidate. It would be a time of reckoning.

"Hello my friends. This is Anastasia Watkins, your proud Congresswoman from Georgia and Washington DC. I am so very happy to have you join me on this call today. I will not keep you long. I know you are busy women. I know you are strong, dedicated, powerful women that are ready to change the world. You are my peers. You are my equals. You have energized me in so many ways. I am here because of

you. I am here with you. I want you to all know how proud I am of everything we have accomplished together over the last five or so years! It has been and will continue to be an amazing time in history.

Our time is here.

I will be seeking the nomination for President of the United States of America in the upcoming 2054 election. I will make a formal announcement to the world in two weeks at the United Environmental Strategy Summit in Washington. Until then, I ask that you wait to make comments about this.

It is likely that there will be a leak of this information. You are smart individuals and I trust you to respond accordingly. I wanted you to be the first to hear the news directly from me. You are the reason I am here and the reason I wish to move forward. It is all for you. And for your daughters and grandchildren and women all over the world that are seeking a better tomorrow.

We may appear to be just simple gray-haired old ladies with not much to offer. But do NOT underestimate our power. Our will. Our strength and tenacity. We WILL prevail. We WILL win back what was taken from us. The world will be better for it. Thank you for all your support. I will be in touch again soon. We have just begun our work! Peace to you all and power to the women."

The call ended and the room erupted in applause for their fearless leader. Anastasia was about to be in tears but kept her composure. She was so proud and so happy at this moment in her life. She gazed around the room and smiled.

"Okay, that is done." "How many people were on the call Abby?"

"Would you believe 3,223." Abby grinned. "I would say that was a success boss."

Anastasia smiled back. "Thank you all. Now we have a lot of work to do ladies. But first I need to talk with Hank. It is time he is brought into the loop. And it is time for you women to share this with your men if you so wish. We are all in this together and the road is going to be a long one. I say we call it a day and meet back here tomorrow ready to take on the world." And with that comment Anastasia gathered her things and made her way out of the door. "Have a good day kids!"

Abby, Leona and Kendall all looked at each other. They told the rest of the office team to go ahead and go home and get some rest. Tomorrow begins the yearlong workday.

The friends sat and talked about the morning. Kendall said she planned to share the call with Chad and explain some of this but probably could not imagine how to explain it all to him. Abby agreed. She has wanted for so long to tell Noah everything. It was time. So today would be the day. Leona said she had already shared all her secrets with her cat years ago. "Cher knows everything already. She is my confidant. I had to tell her. I am sorry." Then they all burst into laughter until tears came running down their cheeks.

Leona asked her friends to call her later and let her know how it went with the men. She then tidied up the office and was about to walk out when Mark Hunter appeared at the front door. He was about to walk in just as Leona pulled the door open to walk out.

"Oh, excuse me Sir. What are you doing here?"

"Hi Leona. I thought I might catch you on your lunch break since it is a little after noon. Do you have time to grab some lunch?"

"Uh, I guess I can do that. I was just leaving for the day. Taking a short day today. What did you have in mind?"

"How about the bar across the street where we met last week?"

"Oh gosh no. The bar food is horrible. The only good thing there is the cold beer and pretzels. How about Pearls down the street? We can walk."

"Sounds good to me."

The walk took about ten minutes and was enough time for Leona to ask the usual questions. Mark said he had an antique piece he dropped off to a customer around the corner so thought he would take a chance of catching her at the office. They got to the bistro and found a nice corner booth. The place was always packed, and this was the only available table.

"So, Mark, what does the rest of your day look like? Don't you have any real estate business today?"

"Oh, I always have real estate stuff. It never ends. I feel like a doctor that is always on call. In fact, I am waiting for a response to an offer we put in today, so I do have to answer my phone if the agent calls me back. I apologize for that. I hope you understand."

"Yes, of course. I am always on call with Anastasia as well. I get it."

"So, you seem to like living in DC. Do you ever miss Atlanta?"

"I always miss Atlanta. And I miss home in Alabama too. My mom is still there. But we visit each other as often as possible."

"I miss Atlanta, just not the slow pace of life there. It is different here. I like the rush of the city and the culture. There is so much to do here! I just haven't made a lot of new friends since I moved here three years ago. It is harder as we are older to meet people. Do you agree?"

"Yes, I do. I am glad I have my friends. And doing this job has brough me lots of acquaintances. Maybe not real close friends. But I have met a lot of new people."

The conversation went longer than Leona expected and before she knew it the clock said 3 pm. She enjoyed Mark and found him interesting. But she needed to get home and work on some things for tomorrow. And she was anxious to meet up with Tucker tonight. They had dinner plans. He told her to dress up because he was taking her somewhere special to celebrate their one-year dating anniversary!

Abby was waiting for Noah to arrive home from work so they could have a nice long talk. She told him she was making dinner for them. She cooked pasta and picked out a nice red wine for Noah. She was missing her wine for sure and was ready not to be pregnant anymore. Only a few months left, she thought.

Abby served up dinner and began to explain what had happened today at the office. Noah was amazed at the story and how many supporters Anastasia had with their secret society thing. He found it all very interesting and was even more proud of his wife. He knew how intelligent she was, and he always understood the bond between these women. He knew they had a mission and he suspected it might include Anastasia running for President one day in the future.

"Wow, you ladies are really something!" "I am quite proud of you girl. I don't know how you will run a campaign with a new baby, but we will figure it out."

"Noah, I don't plan to run anything. Being a mom comes first right now. My friends and co-workers know this. Kendal and Leona are taking the lead with all this, and I will do what I can from home base. But I will need your support. We are in for a wild ride honeybee."

Noah hugged his wife and rubbed her protruding belly. "I love my ladies so much. I will do anything for you. All you have to do is ask."

"Have you thought any more about asking your mom to come and stay for a while? You know she has offered this on several occasions. She is chomping at the bit to come and stay. She wants to help you."

"Yes, I have given it some thought. But we have the baby room to finish, and the other spare room is filled with boxes of junk. We will need to clear it all out and set up a guest room for mom. Can we do all that?"

"I think so. We have some time. I will check into getting us a storage place. We should have done that in the first place. We can figure it all out babe."

"I love you honey."

"I love you too. Now go put your feet up and I will clean up the dishes. Thanks for the great meal. Oh, and call your friends. I know they want an update."

CHAPTER ELEVEN

Leona felt nervous for some reason. Tucker seemed anxious earlier when he asked her about dinner tonight. He usually doesn't make such a big deal about meeting for dinner. Over the last year they have been inseparable. Leona has attended her fair share of political and business events with her new man. And they have shared many days and nights together. Recently they began discussing living together. Tucker has a nice townhouse in DC and Leona has an apartment just outside of town. But with traffic, it takes about thirty minutes or longer to get from one place to the other. They had not landed on any decision, but it was an ongoing conversation.

Tucker arrived to pick up Leona for dinner and he was dressed in a luscious black suit with velvet lapels. He had a single red rose for his date. They drove to a very nice Italian Winery and Restaurant a few miles away. Leona was impressed and she had not heard of the place so that was unexpected.

Dinner was wonderful and there was a pianist playing beautiful music at a grand piano. The place was quiet and only a few guests were there on this Wednesday evening. Leona thought perhaps it was busier on the weekends. She did not know at the time that Tucker reserved a section of the restaurant just for them so he could have some privacy.

Suddenly the wait staff disappeared, and Tucker got down on one knee next to his love. He reached into his jacket and pulled out a small black box and placed it in front of Leona.

"My darling. I cannot tell you how much this last year has meant to me. You entering my life has made me a better man. I am so in love with you, and I cannot imagine my life without you. Our future is going to be a crazy one, I am certain, and I would like you to join me for the ride. I promise to always put you first. Will you be my wife my darling Leona Branson?"

Leona was already in tears and hugging her man. He opened the little box and showed her the most beautiful diamond ring.

"Yes! Yes! A million times yes! I love you too you crazy man. I never want to live another day without you by my side".

Tucker placed the ring on her finger and kissed her ever so gently. Suddenly the wait staff, restaurant owner, bartender and half the restaurant were standing there applauding the couple! The owner brought them a bottle of their best champagne on the house.

The two finished up dinner with chocolate dessert and champagne and took a walk in the vineyard. The night was perfect with a full moon overhead. The breeze was blowing through Leona's long mostly gray hair, and she grabbed it in one hand to hold it down. She was smiling and feeling so wonderful tonight, she hoped this night would never end. Tucker was staring at her with his dark brown eyes. They seemed to look directly into her soul, she thought. He had a way of looking at her that made her feel as though she could melt. She wanted nothing more than to have this man as her partner for life.

On the drive home Leona kept saying "Mrs. Leona Jackson" in her head. It had a nice ring to it, she thought. She was so happy. Her heart was full.

At home the pair began to discuss the future. They drank more wine and talked for hours. They both had such respect for one another and were so happy to have found each other and they wanted the same things in life. Children were discussed and were optional but they both understood it was something they needed to do soon, or their time would pass. Leona was turning forty this year and it did not seem like being pregnant would fit into their life right now. They landed on a wait-and-see attitude and that included the possibility of adoption.

The topic of the wedding came up of course and with the campaign about to kick off there would be little time for a wedding.

"Darling, I know you want the whole shebang of a wedding with lots of plans, rehearsal dinners and live orchestra music, but it just seems like it will not be possible any time soon. I want you by my side during the campaign and I want to call you…my wife."

"Your wife! Oh my gosh, that sure sounds wonderful. But that would mean getting married right away."

"Yes, it would. I am on board if you are. What do you think? Shall we just do it?"

Leona was stunned at the thought but not objective to it. After all, they just married off their friends and were in the midst of baby showers for Noah and Abby. It had all been a lot of planning and frankly Leona was not ready to do all that again any time soon. "Yes, I am in! Let's just go the courthouse and get hitched."

"Well, I thought we could at least have a small ceremony", Tucker suggested to his love. Maybe we can put a small chapel wedding together in a couple of weeks? Your girlfriends can help us pull it off, right?"

The couple decided to go for it. They would make calls tomorrow and see if their parents could be there. Leona would check the office calendar to figure out a good day to make it happen. For now, she would linger for a bit longer just staring at the giant diamond ring glaring from her ring finger. Wow, she thought. This is a big diamond. I am worth it, she thought to herself before heading off to bed.

The morning was not the usual Saturday and the two opted not to take a usual morning run. Instead, they each began making calls to family and friends. They did a zoom call with their mother's and Leona showed off the giant rock on her hand. Her mother was over the top with emotion. She would get a plane ticket as soon as they set the final date.

"Well babe, there is no turning back now. My mother will be telling the entire world that her daughter is finally getting married! So don't you dare change your mind." They both laughed loudly and continued making calls.

Anastasia knew already that Tucker had made these plans. She was excited and eager to clear the calendar for a day that worked for everyone. The girlfriends decided to meet at a local café' for lunch and Leona plopped her hand out onto the table. They all screamed like teenagers and then began to cry happy tears for their friend.

"I cannot believe this!" Kendall was the first to ask the big question. "When can you possibly pull this off?"

"Well, that is the thing. We decided we must do this now instead of later. Later may never come. So, we need to sync up calendars with each of you to find a day in the next couple of weeks to get us hitched!"

The girlfriends were shocked but happy. How would they make this happen? Abby jumped in and agreed wholeheartedly that this was the best plan. After all, there was a baby coming and a presidential campaign to run. Besides that, they should be able to squeeze in a quick wedding for the soon-to-be Vice President of the United States. "Okay then. Let's look at dates."

CHAPTER TWELVE

The day had arrived before she could take a moment to pause and think about it. Leona sat at her breakfast bar in her DC townhouse, staring down at the sparkling diamond ring, wondering what in the world she had gotten herself into. She didn't have cold feet, but she wasn't sure this was the right thing to do. Why now, she thought? Well, she knew the answer to that question. It was now or never in her mind. She was about to turn forty in a couple of weeks. The man she was about to marry today will likely be the new Vice President next year. She will be Mrs. Vice President. She began to shake, and her mother walked into the room.

"Darling, you need to start getting ready for the big day. You only have a couple of hours before we need to head over to the salon and have them do your hair and makeup."

"Mom, am I doing the right thing? I mean I love Tucker with all my heart. He is the most wonderful human I have ever known. But am I worthy of him? Why did he choose me?

Kristen Branson knew exactly why he chose her beautiful, intelligent, stylish, loving daughter! How could he not pick her. "Sweetheart, you two are meant for one another. It is obvious to everyone around you. You are both wonderful humans and you deserve each other. Now go get your big girl panties on and let's get you married!"

Leona thought at that moment she was glad Kristen was her mom. She always knew just what to say to make things better. She had a no-nonsense way about her that made you do what she said. So, Leona finished her last sip of hot tea and got herself ready for the day.

First stop was the salon owned by a friend of Anastasia's that agreed to close and just have the wedding party there for makeup and hair. The three friends met there and exchanged a few laughs before heading out to pick up Leona's suit for the wedding. She had opted for a long skirt and suit jacket with feminine touches of lace and pearls. It was Fall so her color choice was not white, but soft lavender. Leona ordered the designer suit from a friend's boutique. She had to find something ready on the rack as there was no time for anything custom.

There was a small chapel with an attached restaurant that had an outdoor garden patio named *The Chapel Restaurant.* It was perfect for a group of twenty or so. It was kept very quiet from the press and the restaurant closed this Saturday for a "Private Event". This was usual for them, so nothing was suspicious. Anastasia and Hank arrived and parked behind the building. A small alley had been blocked off for the wedding guests to arrive without being seen.

Tucker had a friend that was ordained and would perform the short ceremony. The couple wrote their own vows, and a friend of the group played the guitar.

"My God", was all that was running through the brain of Tucker Jackson as he looked up to see his bride slowly walking toward him. He could not take his eyes off her, and he could feel his heart pounding in his chest. He was so happy, and his heart was full. He knew in this moment that this was the best day of his life so far. He doubted there would ever be anything better.

Kendall and Abby wore darker purple dresses. They found a nice loose-fitting design for the very pregnant Abby. Leona asked her mother to stand up for her as Matron of Honor, which she gladly accepted. Tucker had asked Hank to be his Best Man. The men had been friends for many years now, so it seemed appropriate. All the men wore black suits.

The Chapel Restaurant was lit with candles and large ferns adorned the brick walls. White and purple hydrangeas scattered around the room making it lovely for the short ceremony. There were a handful of Washington who's who in attendance as well as family and friends. They made their way to the outdoor garden for a nice, seated dinner. Tucker insisted on surf and turf, so each guest received a lobster tail and steak, along with a salad, fresh fruit and several choices of side dishes.

Wait staff carried trays of drinks all evening and offered various desert bites. There was a small wedding cake that was boxed and handed to the guests as they departed. The weather was perfect, and the outside heaters Tucker ordered were a hit. The beautiful bride wore a faux white fur cape to keep her warm. It could not have been a more perfect night, thought Leona. She listened as her best friends toasted her and Tucker and wished them well. Abby had to leave early as she told her friends that her ankles were swelling to the size of grapefruit, and she would never be able to take her shoes off if she didn't get home soon.

Tucker had arranged for a private jet to take the newlyweds to Martha's Vinyard for a couple of days. They said their goodbyes and headed to the airport. It was a special day for all these special friends. Leona could not be happier in this moment.

The house that Tucker had rented was a small beach cottage owned by a family friend. What it lacked in size was made up for in charm and design. The house was white inside and out. It was furnished in true Martha's Vinyard style with ocean blue paintings of ships and sailboats, pale green sofas with extra thick cushions you sunk into and could barely escape from. The bedding was luscious and white and there were no less than ten pillows which mostly landed on the floor and stayed there for the entire visit.

The kitchen was stocked with food and beverages and ready-made meals to pop in the oven. Wine and champagne filled the shelves and pastries filled the pantry. There was an old-fashioned record player and stacks of albums to choose from. The couple listened to music and watched the birds on the beach as the waves crashed towards their bungalow each morning and evening for three days. It all went by so quickly and Leona begged Tucker to stay there with her "forever".

"My darling, I would love nothing better than to lay here in this bed with you and take long walks on the beach every day. Just say the word, and I will gladly escape with you."

Leona knew they could not do that, but the idea was so wonderful she could not help but to ask herself if it was possible. Could they just leave everything behind, forget this whole running for office stuff and live a life of leisure here on this beautiful island? She knew the answer. But these few days had been just what she needed to re-charge and get ready for her new life. She was now Mrs. Tucker Jackson. What a thought!

CHAPTER THIRTEEN

Back in DC the town was buzzing about the secret wedding of the town bachelor, Tucker Jackson. It was widely known in political circles that Jackson was a close friend of the Congresswoman, and rumors were already stirring about a presidential bid for Anastasia. Reporters were tracking down information about the new Mrs. Jackson and her background. The phones were ringing off the hook, so to speak, in the Watkins office. Kendall was doing her best with the help of about a dozen interns, to field questions and answer with, "no comment", as often as possible.

Anastasia finally decided a quick press conference was in order before the newlyweds returned to town so they would not be bombarded as soon as their plane landed in DC.

"Ladies and Gentlemen, I thank you for coming…" She went on to explain the wedding that had taken place between her good friends and comrades, and how she appreciated their respect for privacy during this time. She answered questions about why the sudden wedding and speculation of a baby, etc. Anastasia was very straightforward and did not mince words. It was clear this was a wedding between two very busy people that were very much in love. That was it. No other story for now.

Anastasia was not certain her reporter friends accepted her explanations but decided it would have to do for today. She had work to get to and soon enough she would be announcing her bid for office. The event was coming up next weekend where she would make her announcement.

There was already word on the street about a possible announcement at this upcoming convention of environmentalists. There were also stories in various parts of the country about an underground group of women that had plans to take over some businesses. The stories were never quite right, but the word would be out soon, and the race would be on. Anastasia Watkins was ready.

Finally, Leona was back from her quick honeymoon, and they all agreed the "honeymoon was over" and it was time to get to work. In the four days Leona was out of town there had been several press releases about Anastasia Watkins, Tucker Jackson and the rest of the team. Abby was about to have her baby any day now and Noah had enough on his plate at the Art Institute to keep him busy. Noah and Abby decided they needed help, so they invited Sandra James, Abby's mother, to come and stay with them for a while. She had recently retired and loved the idea of getting away and being there for her daughter. Sandra was arriving this weekend and would stay for at least six weeks. The due date was a week away.

Noah had managed to spend every waking minute not at his office, cleaning out the guest room and setting it up as well as putting together baby furniture for the nursery. Kendall and Leona helped with painting and decorating the baby room earlier in the month, so that project was completed. Abby chose a woodland creature's theme for their baby girl. Light pink walks with cutouts of bunnies and birds and baby deer that looked like Bambi. Soft rugs and piles of blankets stacked in the corner along with a swivel chair for rocking the baby, made it all just perfect. Now if this little girl arrived on time all would be fine.

Kendall and Chad with Joe in tow had talked a bit about marriage and decided to just wait. They were in no hurry. They were very much in love, and they knew they would eventually do the marriage thing, but they both had very busy lives that were about to get busier. They agreed that next year they could make plans and include a very long vacation honeymoon, but for now they would carry on and help get their friend elected to the highest office in the land.

Chad had set up a golf trip for the guys as soon as Tucker was back. However, Tucker bailed on them and told the others to go without him. Then Noah also bailed because it looked like the baby may come early. So, it was just Chad and Hank and they decided to go ahead and get in a game and planned a private plane ride down to Palm Coast Florida for a day trip. Anastasia wasn't thrilled because this was a day before her big announcement at the conference. But she agreed Hank should go and have a day of fun. Those days are about to be over soon for the "*First Gentleman*".

Hank liked having his own plane. He had gotten his pilot's license a few years ago. He was used to short trips up and down the coast with his buddies. This was an easy trip to plan. They would fly down in the morning and return in the evening. So, plans were all set.

The guys met at the local air strip where the plane was stored. Anastasia had begged Hank to be careful and to get home tonight so he could go with her to the gala tomorrow. He gave her his usual big grin and told her not to worry. "Wouldn't miss it ma'am! See ya tonight".

The weather was clear although it was a bit cool and soon it would be hard to make these trips in the small plane once the snow started. It was a bit windy today but nothing too concerning. The guys tossed their golf clubs in the back along with a change of clothes in case they needed them. The traffic controller gave them the all clear and they set off for Florida. They were flying near the eastern coastline and the trip would be about an hour and a half.

Anastasia was collaborating with her team on her speech for the event tomorrow. They had all met at the office to go over talking points. It was going to be a big day. The press had been alerted that a big announcement was coming from the Senator, so everyone was on high alert. DC was buzzing about the upcoming election next year and most had decided Watkins would be in the race.

Abby's mother arrived and settled in with her daughter and Noah. She loved her guest suite, and the nursery was so cute. "Oh, my goodness, you kids have outdone yourself. How did you get all this done?"

Noah was quick to accept the praise and thanked her for noticing. Abby laughed at him as her mom winked at her. "Men love getting praised. You can stop now Mom." They all laughed, and Abby doubled over in pain. "Oh my God, that hurt!" Abby yelled out. "Crap!" And just then, her water broke, and her mother yelled for Noah to grab a towel. "Sit down dear, you are in labor." "Noah, call your doctor and order us a car to get to the hospital."

Noah began running from room to room as if he was looking for something. "What are you looking for dear?"

"My phone!" Of course, his phone was in his hand as he shouted this across the room. "Where is my phone?" And then Abby cried out again, "Oh wow, this is serious. I am not sure I am ready for this. Mom, you just got here. I am not due for another week. What does this mean Mom?"

"Well, it means the baby wants to meet her grandma now instead of next week dear. It is okay. We will take care of you. Now go get your hospital bag ready while I help calm your husband."

Noah finally found his phone in his hand, took a couple of deep breaths, and called the doctor. They told him to come on to the hospital now since the water had broken. Then he looked at Abby and told her he loved her. "It is okay honey, we got this. I got you."

Abby texted her friends once they were at the hospital. "Well ladies, it is happening…we are at the hospital now. Mom will update you. No need to come here until we know more. I am fine. Damn this hurts."

Leona and Kendall were so excited. Anastasia said she figured Abby would try to upstage her. "That girl will go extra lengths for attention." They all laughed. "I guess we are done talking about my speech tomorrow. Go on and get out of here. Go be with your friend. I will text Hank and let him know the scoop."

Anastasia sent a text to Hank, but he did not reply. She assumed he was flying and about to be in Florida, so she didn't expect to hear from him right away. She thought about Abby and worried for her.

She will stop by the hospital later tonight to check on her. Surely by then the baby will be here.

Hank and Chad were talking about golf and how life was about to change for all of them. Chad saw the text from Anastasia. So, after talking it over with his co-pilot friend they decided to forget about the golf and head back home to be with the ladies. They knew Noah was outnumbered and would need them. Hank spoke to the traffic controller about his change of flight plan and how he was turning back to DC. They warned him about a bad wind stream behind him and suggested he not turn around but to land and go back later. Hank insisted they needed to make the turn, so he headed his plane back to the north and began to head home. Suddenly, just outside of North Carolina they picked up 100 mph winds that tossed the small plane around like a beach ball. The plane began rocking severely and Hank told Chad to "hang on buddy, it is getting rough, but we can make it", so Chad grabbed onto the seat and tightened his seatbelt. "Are you so sure", he shouted as the plane continued to rock. Then the plane, without warning, took a nosedive and began to descend towards the dark blue sea below them.

"Mayday, mayday, mayday…. may need a sea rescue gentlemen. We are headed down." And within seconds the plane was diving into the ocean, nose first, spinning as she fell. Chad and Hank spun around with the metal plan and seatbelts held them into their seats or they would have died on impact. This particular plane had the latest safety windshield that could withstand the impact of a sea crash. After a few minutes Chad realized he was alive and inside the plane that was intact and still diving to the sea floor below. Oxygen masks had dropped down and he placed one on his face. He looked over to see Hank unconscious and placed a mask on his face for him. "Hank, wake up, man don't leave me now. I need you man. Oh my God. You have to wake up!" Chad was shaking his friend and looking around in disbelief that the plane was not yet filling with water. How was it possible? Maybe I am dead, he thought. "Hank, wake up!"

Just then Hank started to move. It took a minute before he realized where he was and what was happening. "Oh man. I am sorry buddy. Okay, let's get out of here."

"What do you mean? How can we get out of here? We will die if we open the door. Shit."

"No, we won't die Chad. Listen to me. This plane is special. Equipped for this kind of thing. I have a special life preservation system on board. We have wet suits, flares, and a turbo powered rescue torpedo. Just follow my lead. We will be okay. Damn my head hurts." Hanks's seatbelt had partially torn loose so he had taken an impact to his head and blood was trickling down his face. Chad thought he would vomit and was shaking uncontrollably but his bloody friend seemed calm as he spoke out orders. "Put this suit on, attach the clip from the torpedo, follow my lead and do it NOW, we must move fast if we want to make it."

The traffic controller back at the tower was looking for the lost plane. He called his team leader over to tell him about the flight and what had happened. "I think they went down Sir. Looks like they are off radar and under water. Shall we send rescue and recovery now?"

"Who are the bodies on board?"

"Captain Hank Watkins and a Mr. Chadwick Turner, both from DC. Isn't that the Congresswoman's husband?"

"Hell yes. But he has a damn good plane and is a hell of a pilot, so his chances are good. Let's go find them."

Back in DC the friends have gathered at the hospital and are awaiting the arrival of baby Constantine. They weren't sure what name Noah and Abby had landed on? Last they discussed it was either going to be Angelina or Casandra. Suddenly Noah appeared and said the baby was here. "We are naming her Casandra Elaina Constantine. She is perfect. Six pounds and one ounce and 18 inches long."

"She has lots of black hair and came out yelling loudly."

"Oh, and Abby is doing great too. She is a trooper."

The group of friends erupted in cheers. Noah headed back to be with his wife. Abby's mother came out to sit with them and give them all the details. As they sat there in the waiting room the story came across on the television about a downed plane carrying the husband of Senator Watkins and a friend. Leona and Kendall saw the story at the same time. Kendall stared at the screen and her face went pale. She began to shake in disbelief. "What? What the hell? Chad? Hank? Am I seeing that right? What?"

"Calm down honey. We don't have the entire story yet. They are probably safe somewhere already. Let me make some calls."

Leona called Tucker first. He answered and gave her the information he had. He was on his way to the hospital. She hung up and called Anastasia. No answer. Then a text came through from Anastasia. "Plane crashed near South Carolina and rescue is searching for them. I am on the phone now with the Coast Guard. Call later."

"Crap" – "Okay, Anastasia is talking to the Coast Guard to get details. The plane did crash, and this is all we know for now honey."

Kendall was losing it. In a flash second, she went from being happy about the birth of her best friend's child to hearing her fiancé may be at the bottom of the ocean. It was more than she could manage, and she began to cry and could not stop.

Noah and Leona decided not to tell Abby anything for now. Not until they had more details.

Anastasia knew about the plane and the special safety windshield and the rescue equipment on board just for this kind of emergency. This gave her some comfort, but not enough. She wasn't certain of anything at that moment. She needed her sweet husband to be found alive and brought back to her. She could not go on without him in her life. She prayed and made calls to everyone that would listen and provide some kind of assistance. She used every connection she had to get the rescue teams out there searching for Hank and Chad. She would find them and bring them back. She hopped on a charter plane and headed to the nearest Coast Guard office where the search was being conducted. Then she called Kendall to talk to her and try to calm her friend.

Anastasia was escorted by her security detail and arrived in North Carolina at the Coast Guard office. She was a force to be reckoned with, especially during a crisis. She came in with authority and was very much aware of her surroundings. "Who is in charge here please?" "Anastasia Watkins here, you are searching for my husband I believe?"

"Yes ma'am. Officer Martin here. We have a chopper in the air and three boats on the surface where we believe the plane went down. Our search area is about 100 square miles, but the wind is making it difficult to maneuver out there."

"Were they headed south?" she asked with authority. "No ma'am. For some reason Captain Watkins decided to turn around and head back north to DC. Said it was an emergency family situation and he had to turn around." "Ma'am, he got a warning from the tower about the wind. We suggested he not turn around. There was a bad current coming across just as he made his turn. It must have caught the plane and tossed it around. Sorry ma'am. But that is what we know."

"Okay, so do you know about the plane? It is equipped with…." "Yes ma'am", he cut her off. We understand the place should survive the impact and if the pilot and his passenger are able to use the safety tank, they could possibly make it out alive."

"Of course, the pilot knows how to use the tanks. He is the one that helped design the damn things. Sorry gentlemen, it has been a long day. That is my husband and our best friend out there. Please help me find them."

"Yes ma'am. Congresswoman Watkins, we are at your service ma'am. Happy to help. We are on it and will do our very best to find them."

Tucker and Leona sat at the hospital doing their best to comfort Kendall. They got regular updates from Anastasia to pass along. Finally, they were all able to visit Abby and see the new baby girl. It helped to ease the pain for Kendall, but she finally had to go home and wait by the phone for any update. Abby was brought up to speed on what had happened. She was upset of course and tried to comfort her friend. They did their best to be happy for Abby and Noah, but it was a bittersweet day. Abby held her baby girl extra tight that night and prayed for her friends. Tomorrow would be a better day, she thought.

Abby texted some with Anastasia and sent her a photo of the baby to comfort her. Noah would not leave her side that night and decided to sleep at the hospital.

"Chad, when I say go, you pull this ring. We each have our tank that will pull us to the surface. It works at a set speed, so we do not rise too quickly. Don't panic if it slows or stops for a moment. It is designed for that. Trust that you have enough oxygen to last while we safely ascend to the surface. We can do this. By now the rescue teams are out there waiting for us. I will see you at the top buddy. Now, go!"

Chad hung on tight to the heavy rope tied to the end of a tank with a small propellor and a headlight. He could see a few feet around him as he was being pulled up to the surface. It seemed like a long ride but in fact only took about six minutes to surface. The rescue torpedo shot up out of the water pulling Chad with it then crashed back and floated there. Hank's tank came crashing through the surface seconds later. The two men were bobbing there several feet apart and managed to swim towards one another. The water was not calm, and the waves caused them to bob up and down and they each found it difficult to hold steady.   Hank had lost enough blood to make him feel dizzy. He was bobbing around and appeared to Chad to be losing consciousness. "Wake up Hank", Chad yelled loudly. The water was cold and wild, and the pair bobbed and shook like fishing bobs, Chad thought. "Keep calm. Look for the coastguard", Chad kept saying to himself.

Back at the pier office the captain in charge was giving Anastasia an update. It was dark now and the rescue teams were about to call it a night. Two of the boats had turned back and the helicopter was on the dock. Maps were being synchronized to reflect the search areas they had covered for the past two hours before sunset. The coast guard was advising that search teams would go back out at sunrise.

"Sorry fella's but that last boat is staying out there until you find my husband. I have the authority to make that happen. Do you understand?" "If we wait for morning, they could surface tonight and drift many miles or be consumed by the sea. Hank knows what he is doing. They will be on the surface soon."

Anastasia was telling herself all would work out, but she was not a hundred percent certain of that. If the windshield failed, there was no hope. They would have died upon impact. But her crazy husband convinced her to spend thousands of dollars last year to add this special life-saving shield so that would not happen. Let's hope it was worth it, she thought. And she waited.

Anastasia looked up and there stood Kendall Otana, her dear friend. She looked horrible. "Well, you are a sight for sore eyes. How the hell did you get here?"

"I had to jump on a plane. I could not sit at home and wait another second. Have they had any luck yet?"

"Dear, I expect to see our guys any minute now. I wouldn't let the last boat come back without them. You will see. I just know they are going to come home to us."

The women hugged and just held one another for a long time.

The water-logged men could see a boat off in the distance with search lights moving across the ocean surface. Hank screamed out to Chad "I told you they would be here looking for us. I have a flare. Hang on buddy". Hank popped the flare from his vest, and it shot up in the air lighting the sky red. The coast guard boat could see the men from the lights in the sky and came roaring towards them. Chad thought they were about to run over them, when suddenly they stopped and bobbed there on the waves. Two divers immediately jumped into the water with life rings and tossed them towards the men. They each held on tight as they were pulled onto the boat.

And then it happened. The boat was coming back to the pier. "I told you not to come back without Hank! Why are they coming back?"

"Ma'am, we have him. They are on the boat."

Both women jumped up and began to run towards the pier. The light was getting closer. They could make out several shapes of men sitting on the boat. Was it really them?

It was! "Oh my God in heaven. Hank! Baby! Oh my God."

"Chad! You are alive! You crazy man. Thank you, Lord!"

The three rescuers jumped off the boat first followed by Hank and Chad. Both men had big smiles on their faces and reached out for their mates. They hugged for a long time and made their way back to the office to complete reports and get checked out by the EMT.

Other than being scared to death and a slight concussion for Hank, the two were in fair condition. Hank had taken a harder hit to his chest and needed oxygen. The men had made it to the surface an hour earlier and just floated in the dark cold waters, so hypothermia had begun to set in. They each needed to have a medical checkup.

"I am sorry honey", said Hank. "I told you that damn windshield and rescue tank were worth it!" She just nodded and agreed. "Kiss me darling. I love you."

"Chad, you had me scared to death."

"You! I was scared shitless. I mean, we actually nose-dived a plane into the ocean and walked away without a scratch. Crazy. I think I am ready to go home babe. I love you so much."

"We will stop at the hospital first and make certain you are both good to go", said Anastasia. They agreed that would be okay.

Back in DC the news was coming across the screens about the rescue and photos of the friends popped up on every website and television. Noah woke up Abby to tell her the good news. They held each other and cried. Everyone in Congress was glad to hear the news and Anastasia was in the spotlight once again. What would the world think tomorrow when she makes her announcement, she wondered?

After a quick checkup at the local hospital and against doctors order the men were released into the care of their ladies. Both were ordered to rest for a week before any stressful activities.

"Can we go home now honey? I must announce that I am running for president tomorrow, so I need a good night's sleep." The friends all laughed at that thought and they made their way home in a small charter plane.

"Can we fly over land if you don't mind?" Chad asked the pilot with a smile.

CHAPTER FOURTEEN

Kendall and Chad got to sleep around 2:00am and the alarm sounded at 6:00am. They looked at each other and decided they could lay there motionless and just hold one another for another thirty minutes, so they did just that. They were both exhausted from the prior day events. Chad was completely wiped out and decided he would take a few days off work. Kendall wanted to do the same, but she had no choice but to attend this gala tonight with her boss. The two of them could never have imagined the life they were living at this moment. But they were happy to be together. Joe the dog jumped into the bed and demanded kisses and to be taken for his morning walk. "He's your dog honey." With that Chad got up and slipped into his sweatpants and hoodie while Joe jumped around him whining with joy for his master. Chad thought in that moment he really was just glad to be alive. Those words were never truer.

"Come on Joe. Let's go see what the world has to offer us today." Kendall got a quick shower and was ready to leave for the office when the boys returned from their walk. "Goodbye honey. I am sorry I must leave you. I will be home around three to get ready for tonight. Try to rest a bit and I will see you soon. Love you babe!"

Joe had his walk and now breakfast to be followed by a long nap. Chad ate a bite and began having flashbacks from yesterday. He could not stop shaking. He began to break out in a cold sweat. He decided a hot shower would calm his nerves. Maybe a couple of aspirins wouldn't hurt. He downed the pills with juice then lingered in the shower longer than usual. Most of the hot water was drained before Chad could bring himself to step back out of the shower into the real world. He felt uneasy and his nerves were shot. Did he almost die yesterday? Of course he did. Why did he live? What is my purpose in life, he thought. Chad just sat on the edge of the bed petting his friend and wondering about life and death. He was able to drift back into sleep for another hour before waking to try again to start his day. He could do it. He had to be there for his friends tonight and show Kendall he was going to be okay. She needed him now more than ever. It was going to be a long hard year ahead of them.

The phone rang and it was Noah calling. "Hey man, you are alive!"

"Yep, sorry about that. You aren't getting rid of me that easy." Noah told his friend he was so glad he was okay, and he hoped to see him tonight.

"Are you attending the gala without Abby? When is she bringing the baby home?"

"Yes, she insisted that I go in her place so I can give her all the details of the night. She is staying in the hospital until tomorrow. The baby girl is a little jaundice, so they want to watch her one more day. They are both doing great though, and I am so excited to be a dad!"

"We will see you there tonight. Love you man."

"Love you too brother. I mean that."

Kendall and Leona were busy making final changes to the speech for Anastasia. Tucker stopped by to visit Hank this morning after Anastasia left for the office. Hank was glad to have the company.

Tucker brought pastries and coffee and the two men talked for a couple of hours about everything that had happened.

"Hank, you are about to go on a wild ride. It might be crazier than crashing your plane into the ocean."

"I doubt that. But I am ready. I know once Anastasia makes her speech tonight, my life will never be the same. What the heck is a *First Gentleman* anyway?"

"I am not sure about the Gentleman part, but I think you will just do whatever your wife asks of you."

"Well, I do that now my friend!"

The friends knew that changes were coming, but they had no idea just how much was in store for them.

"See you tonight, Sir. Don't forget the little people!"

Mark Hunter stopped by the office to check on everyone. He wanted to give his support to Anastasia and told her he would be at the gala. He smiled at the ladies and made his way out. Leona still wasn't sure about him. There was something about him and she just couldn't put her finger on it. She decided she didn't have time to think about it longer and got on with her day.

Abby was enjoying time with her little Casandra. She decided to call her Cassie. Her mother, Sandra, was thrilled that the name was a nod to her. Sandra stayed all day helping with the baby and with her daughter. Abby was doing well and was really mad she was missing the big event tonight. Noah agreed to live stream it for her.

Everyone that mattered attended the event. It was a fundraiser for the environment and proceeds were going towards improving the parklands around the DC area. This was a huge part of Anastasia's platform. She had raised more money than any other politician in history to help curb global warming. And her efforts have been paying off in recent years. This was the perfect event for her announcement.

Dinner was served and during dessert the speeches began. It took an hour or so to get to the main event of the night. Hank had attended many of these events and had introduced his wife on several occasions. He was a little shaky tonight and still had a headache from his mild concussion but refused to give this task to anyone else.

"Ladies and Gentlemen and special guests this evening. We welcome you and thank you for your support." Before he could get another word out the applause began. The crowd of 300 or so people stood up and clapped for Hank. There were shouts and whistles from the crowd. "Woo Hoo! Glad to have you alive!"

Others shouted out as well and Hank blushed a little at the outpouring of sympathy and love from his DC friends. After composing himself he continues with a very fine introduction of his wife. "I give you, your Senator, Congresswoman, and my fine wife, Anastasia Watkins!"

The crowd roared again. Everyone in the room knew something great was coming. Noah was live streaming the speech for Abby. Leona and Tucker were front and center along with Kendall and Chad and all their parents that were able to attend.

Anastasia walked out onto the stage with her long gray hair flowing and her big smile lighting up the room. She brough energy to the room as usual. She was stunning in her long black dress and diamond earrings. She always knew how to wear just enough jewelry, but never too much. Just enough makeup, but not too much, and the shoes were always perfect.

As she spoke with grace and excitement about our planet and the future, all ears were on her. Cameras were snapping as reporters lined the walls. Finally came her moment. The moment. She stared out at the room in front of her, nodded her head slightly, then lifted her head high with a huge smile.

"Dear friends and colleagues, I am so happy to share with you tonight that I would like to be your next President of the United States! I will be running for office and would like your support as I begin my journey!"

She could not get in another word. The noise level in the room was shattering. Anastasia tried to continue her speech, but it was not happening. She managed a few more words then kindly said "thank you so much for your support" and she made her way to the side of the stage. Hank met her halfway and walked out and they put their hands together and raised them high. Confetti poured from the rafters of the ballroom, and everyone continued to cheer. It was a crazy night. Kendall and Leona ran up on the stage and hugged their friend.

"These are my people!" Anastasia yelled to the crowd. "They will help us get there!" Everyone applauded a bit longer until they could clap no more.

Noah was sending it all live to Abby who was shouting from her bed at the hospital. The nurses were gathered around watching it from her tablet. Finally, the news was breaking on CNN and all programing was interrupted to bring the "breaking news" out of DC.

At the same time as this event, there were about a hundred other private events around the country being led by the *Gray-Haired Ladies* groups. By late evening the news media was so stunned at what was happening, they were not sure what to report.

"We are not sure how this Congresswoman managed to plan all of this or who these people are, but it seems there is some kind of cult following for this lady."

Local and national news was showing parties breaking out across the country. Everyone was scurrying around trying to figure out what was happening. Several of the groups spoke out about how they had been supporting causes backed by the Senator for several years and they were ready to continue their support to get to the Whitehouse. There were fireworks in Atlanta, New York, Denver, Los Angeles and Georgia. The internet was streaming live broadcasts from a dozen cities across the US. It was like nothing the US citizens had ever seen before and it was amazing.

By morning the Watkins team was exhausted but energized. They were amazed by the *Secret Society of Gray-Haired Women* that was no longer a secret! The women came out in force and made their mark on history last night. Anastasia Watkins and her women announced that change was coming, and the time was now. The media had jumped in with both feet and covered it all from sea to shining sea. Headlines across the nation spelled it out plainly…

"Women Come Out in Force…"

"Watkins For Women"

"Secret Society makes itself known."

"This looks like the year for Women."

Instead of everyone running to the office today, they all decided to meet at the hospital. The group of friends arrived in time to escort their friend and her new baby home from the hospital. Anastasia arranged for a police escort for Abby and her family. At the house there was food and flowers and baby gifts from the group.

Abby and Noah were so grateful for such a wonderful bunch of friends. They all looked at the sweet baby girl with her future ahead of her and were excited to be part of making the world a better place for her.

"Cheers to little Cassie and her mom and dad and of course to Grandma Sandra…the best is yet to come!"

They had their champagne toast and left the new little family to get settled at home. There was work to do now and at least a dozen news stations awaiting a call back from Anastasia to do an interview. Leona and Kendall had their work cut out for them. Before leaving they reminded Abby that she could work from home whenever she was ready!

Women all over the world were taking notice of what was happening in the US. Suddenly all eyes were on the Congresswoman, along with her husband, and of course, Tucker Jackson, since he seemed to be everywhere that Anastasia was recently. He had not yet been formally announced as the running mate and they would wait for the actual nomination day to put that out there. However, the media had already figured it out and were following the team very closely.

Women that had been secretly meeting behind closed doors were now out in the open and speaking publicly about their support of Anastasia for President. The lid was off this kettle and there was no stopping the snowball that was more like an avalanche of support.

Over the coming weeks, the media was on full coverage of every move made by Anastasia and her team. *The Society of Gray-Haired Women* was no longer "secret" and along with support came the obvious threats against them. Would-be candidates bidding for office and the usual conservatives were also showing up in force to try and stop the obvious women's movement to take the Whitehouse and control the government. Now that we were in the 2050's, there had been a lot of change in who were the voters of today. Many of the extremists from the 2020's and 2030's had been put to rest or have now been laid to rest. The new era of men was more understanding of the power of women in politics. In fact, there was a woman CEO of the Auto Workers Union and of the NFL. It was definitely a new day and Congress now has 50% women holding a seat at the table.

Mark Hunter was back in the picture working his way into the campaign headquarters. A new office had opened for Anastasia outside of downtown DC so there was enough space to work, and Anastasia had called upon her Realtor friend, Mark, to find the location and get her set up. From there, he managed to get involved in managing the office space and getting equipment and other items needed for local meetings and events. Leona was still not sure about Mark and was keeping a close eye on him.

It had been two weeks since the horrible plane crash that injured Hank and shook-up Kendall's world with the thoughts of losing Chad. All the friends had been through a lot recently and the media was not helping with the continued reporting about the crash and the new Presidential candidate. It was a lot.

Hank had been having daily headaches since the crash and was certain they would be going away soon. He had taken some time away from his business to get some rest and help as he could with kicking off his wife's campaign. He was finding it more difficult in the last few days to concentrate on anything. He was not sleeping well and did not have much appetite for food. It appeared to Anastasia that Hank was dropping weight and acting lethargic. She made an appointment for him to see a specialist and get a follow-up CT scan as his primary doctor suggested.

Hank did not like doctors. He was stubborn and Anastasia was certain he would not want to go so she set it all up then just told Hank he had to go.

"Darling, you must do this. Do it for me please so we can put all this behind us. You know you cannot attend events with me and help with the campaign if these headaches continue. I am worried about you dear. I need you."

Anastasia meant this. She needed this man more than ever. The last few days she had been thinking about the last ten years with Hank. She had met Hank in Law School in Atlanta. They hit it off right away and dated for about a year before they both got too busy with careers to spend much time together. They communicated for a couple of years longer and neither of them had a steady person in their life. Anastasia got her job at the DA's office and worked her way up to the lead District Attorney position. Hank managed to become partners in a very successful law firm in town and the two attended the same events and dinner parties for another year or so before finally starting to date again.

Hank became the one person Anastasia could trust and she told him all her personal secrets about her life and her family and struggles with depression as a teenager. The pair became inseparable in their late twenties and finally were married the year they both turned thirty. They had been married now for fifteen years and would be forty-five this year. They decided at some point that children were not a necessity for them, and their busy life did not allow them to drop everything and raise a child. They loved children and each had several nieces and nephews, and that filled their hearts.

There had been difficult times with each of their careers and family matters that brought them closer together. They had learned to think as one person and finish one another's sentences on most occasions. They did everything together, but also understood the importance of being their own person with their own friends. They allowed space in the relationship, and it was one built on trust. Hank filled all the spaces in Anastasia's heart. He brought strength, but also softness and caring and a warmth she found nowhere else. She knew she was who she was because of this man, her husband, her best friend, her rock. Seeing Hank ill and restless was not usual. They had to get to the bottom of all this and now. She could not take another day of seeing him in pain.

Hank did what he had to do and made his way to the examination that week. They decided on a full body scan to include extra images of the brain due to the recent concussion. Hank had also suffered a severe blow to his chest on impact during the crash. While Chad's seatbelts and other equipment worked well, the belts and pads on the pilot's seat had failed and Hank took a much harder blow to his body than his friend. The bruises were just starting to heal around his ribcage and shoulders.

After a day of tests and scans the doctor asked Hank and Anastasia to step into his office.

"Well, there are some things on the scan we don't like to see. I want to admit you Hank for further tests and some new drugs to clear up what we believe is a blood clot in your brain."

"Blood clot! What?!"

Anastasia said nothing. And she squeezed her husband's hand and told him to hear the doctor out. Both she and Hank were trembling slightly at this moment.

"Yes, but not a usual type of clot that would cause a stroke or anything like that. But it is concerning none-the-less, so we need to deal with it urgently. I am admitting you now and we will do another set of scans and bring in another expert for clarification. If all goes well, we will have you back on your feet and out of here in a few days."

"Well, I guess I don't have a choice here then?"

"Not if you want to live to see your wife as President of the United States sir." The doctor smiled at Hank. They had known one another for a couple of years and Hank knew when his friend was being serious, and this seemed to be one of those times.

Anastasia was squeezing the blood from his hand. "Darling, I may need that hand in the future if you could just loosen your grip a bit.' He smiled at his love. "It is going to be just fine. I am not going to let a little blood clot slow me down. Doc here is going to fix it. So, I need you to let them get me settled in and you can go home and get some rest."

"I am not going anywhere. I will go home when I am good and ready."

"Actually, with respect Mrs. Watkins…. uh Congresswoman Watkins, we will need to get a few more scans done quickly then we can get Hank in a room. It is probably best if you go do what you need to do and come back in about a couple of hours or so. Then you can stay as long as you wish, and we will have more answers for you."

Anastasia looked at Hank with such loving and sad eyes, Hank thought, as he gazed back into her eyes. They did not say a word, but they understood one another clearly. She hugged him and gave him a kiss. The doctor walked out of the room and called for his nurse.

"I will be back in two hours honey. Don't you leave until I get back." They smiled at one another, and Hank hugged his love again and reassured her that all was going to be fine. His head was splitting at this moment, and he was glad to be at the hospital so he could get some help. Hank was admittedly scared about all of this, and he sat back down in the hard wooden chair and dropped his head into his hands and waited for the nurse to fetch him.

CHAPTER FIFTEEN

Anastasia was back at her home without her love. That was the hardest thing she had done in a long while. She asked herself how she could manage to leave him there alone. The presidential candidate sent her entourage of aids and security to leave her alone for the evening. She plopped down onto the sofa and kicked off her shoes. Then, one by one, she called her team, her friends, her family, and told them what was happening with Hank. She had her aids speaking with the hospital staff about privacy and hoped she could keep the media away for at least a day. For now, she just needed to rest so she poured a small glass of red wine and drank it quickly. She set an alarm for sixty minutes and pulled the throw blanket over her shivering body and tried to sleep. She asked her friends not to text her back until she reached out to them later that night and they did as they were asked.

Of course, the entire team of friends were calling one another and texting and trying to decide what to do. They decided to do nothing, and it was business as usual for the rest of the day. Everyone was exhausted from the last two weeks but there was business to do so they got to doing it. That is what Anastasia would want.

Leona was busy following up with the hospital staff about privacy and looking over a comments page to send to Anastasia when it was time to talk with the press. This story would come out soon. Most likely by tomorrow there will be reporters calling. They needed to stay ahead of the press and put a positive spin on this.

Abby was already doing campaign work from home and her mom was a great help with baby Cassie. Noah and Abby had been talking about how wonderful it was to have Sandra staying with them. Of course, Abby loved her mother's help, but she was somewhat surprised how well she was getting along with Noah. The three of them had settled into a rhythm with baby feedings and diaper changes. And they took turns getting up during the night. Noah was first to approach the subject of asking Sandra to come live with them. He brought it up to Abby and they had been talking the last couple of days about how this might work for all of them. Noah also had an idea that might sweeten the deal for Sandra who loved her volunteer work back in Alabama at a local Art Studio. He had an opening at his gallery for a part-time position helping set up gallery openings at the Art Institute. He could ask Sandra about doing that job and helping with Cassie a couple of days a week. Abby could work from home a couple of days each week and Noah could stay home on Fridays. It seemed like a perfect plan.

Abby was on board but wanted to see how things went for the next week or so before deciding to ask her mom about making a permanent move. They also were considering a possible move to a larger home so there were a few moving parts if they were to make this work.

Chad heard the news about Hank, and he knew they were all supposed to wait for Anastasia to call but he had to stop by the hospital, so someone was there with his friend. He told Kendall his plan and agreed he would let her know if there was anything to report.

At the hospital, Chad was able to get one of the charge nurses to give him a few details. All he knew was Hank was finished with scans and getting settled into a room so she would call him when he could go back for a visit.

Chad waited for almost an hour then was told that Hank was sent to ICU and no visitors were allowed. They were communicating with Anastasia, and he would need to speak with her. Chad immediately called Kendall to let her know the latest. She talked with Leona and together they decided to go to the hospital and hope to see Anastasia there. As asked, they did not call their friend. They knew she would call them soon with an update.

Anastasia had been startled by her alarm after sixty minutes of sleep. She managed to really sleep but jumped up from her nap and made her way to the shower to try and shake off the stress and get herself together. She was dressed and out the door within thirty minutes.

On her way back to the hospital the doctor called.

"Anastasia, this is Doctor Langdon. The scans helped us find the exact location of the bleed in Hank's brain. To drain it we must put him into a medically induced coma, insert the stent, and allow several hours for the blood to drain. Hank will be in no pain. We are hopeful this will be resolved completely within 24-48 hours. Do you have any questions?"

"Oh my God, yes, I have lots of questions and I am on my way to the hospital now. Are you there now? May I meet with you in fifteen minutes?"

"Yes, come to my office and we can discuss all of this. Hank is in ICU now and is awake and comfortable, but you will not be able to see him for a little bit. Once we have met and gone over the details you can see Hank before the procedure begins. I will see you shortly.

Anastasia was back in full on stress mode again. She was feeling suddenly out of control of her life. Her sweet husband, her soul mate, he needed her now more than ever. And she needed him. "Driver, please speed up and get me to the hospital as fast as possible."

Anastasia went directly to the doctor's office where he was waiting along with two other physicians. "Congresswomen Watkins, this is Dr. Neal and Dr. Kane, they are extremely capable neurosurgeons that have been assisting me with your husbands care."

The trio of experts went on to clearly explain everything to Anastasia and she was sure she heard almost a third of what they had said. It all sounded terribly complicated and made to seem like a simple process so as not to worry her. Anastasia asked a few questions then insisted on seeing Hank before they put him to sleep.

Walking into the intensive care unit Anastasia was stopped in the hallway by a reporter that had already gotten the scoop about her husband being in ICU. She gave the young reporter a look and said nothing. She held up a hand to say "not now" without saying a word and continued to walk away.

"Hank, my darling. I am here. I met with your doctors, and they seem to have a wonderful plan that involves you getting a couple of days of great sleep."

Hank began to laugh a little and smiled at her. His sweet eyes said it all. The love was there. The fear was also there and the need to hold on to his darling wife for dear life. "This is serious stuff I guess." Hank reached out and Anastasia fell into his arms. They held each other close and steered clear of the IV lines and various wires already attached to the patient.

"My gosh, you are really plugged in my dear. I am sorry you must go through all this honey."

"I am fine Annie…." Hank said Annie in only the dearest moments. No one else ever called her that.

The two of them discussed what was happening and promises were made to be there on the other side of all of this. Paperwork was signed and they discussed their living will. Hank's brother had arrived, and he was able to step in and see Hank for a few minutes. Their mother was in California and not able to make the trip so quickly and would be in town tomorrow. There was no waiting for this procedure. It had to happen at once for the best outcome. Everyone, including Hank, understood.

The friends that had gathered in the waiting room were given a private room with a television screen. They could see Hank via a live streaming screen, and he could see them. This was the only visit allowed so the friends each said something sweet to their dear friend before he was medicated. Most of them were holding back tears and they said their "see you tomorrow" goodbyes. Anastasia was crying now and trying to be strong, but it was a lot. Hank assured her he would have sweet dreams of her wearing that little black bikini she wore to Bora Bora last year and with that comment the nurses began the countdown to place Hank in a medicated coma.

CHAPTER SIXTEEN

Around the country the news was spreading about Hank Watkins being in a coma. What would this do to the bid for the presidency for Anastasia? Reporters were having a field day with the news and various groups had begun to gather outside the hospital and around the Watkins campaign headquarters.

Kendall and Leona were at the office fielding questions and calls. A statement was released that only said *"The Congresswoman's husband was placed in a medically induced coma to drain a blood clot from his brain that was caused by a recent concussion. Watkins is expected to give the press an update in the next 48 hours and has asked for privacy currently."*

The ladies were worried about their friends, and they agreed to just close up shop and go home early today so they could be there if Anastasia needed anything. Mark agreed to stay behind at headquarters and field calls and was instructed to say "no comment" to reporters.

Things had been heating up in the political arena and a couple of opponents of Watkins were stirring up trouble for the Senator. One such rival was the Governor of Michigan, Robert Jameson. He had also recently announced his bid for the presidency this term and he was as conservative as they come these days. The Watkins team knew Jameson would jump all over this recent medical issue for their candidate. He did not disappoint, and immediately began making statements to the press about how Watkins would be "a non-issue soon" because she would need to focus on the "failing health" of her spouse which Jameson insisted should take precedent over her campaigning.

This flurry of press releases managed to heat up the Watkins campaign supporters. The Gray-Haired Ladies were coming out in force again in support of their leader and the news was showing female CEO's and other well respected business leaders touting the "strength of Anastasia Watkins in times like these". Jameson was made out to be a coward making the comments he had made, and the public was asked to stand behind Watkins and her family in a time of need.

The media managed to make Jameson out to be a clown and the support for Watkins was growing steadily.

Other conservatives were touting that Watkins did not understand the "power of prayer" and because of this, her husband would "never make it alive". Media frenzies were everywhere. Several spiritual leaders stepped up to criticize Watkins and called her a "non-believer" and they supported Jameson and would pray for him. Anastasia managed to scroll through her news feeds while sitting in the hospital awaiting the outcome of her husband's procedure. She was saddened by the comments of some people in leadership positions that would use her husband's trauma for political support.

The whole world made Anastasia sad today. Her heart was breaking, and her world felt like it was crumbling before her eyes. Nothing mattered now. Only that Hank survive this medical crisis and come back to her. She bowed her head into her hands, and she prayed for her love to return to her. If he needed her to pull out of the presidential race, she would do it. Hank mattered more to her than anything in the world.

Abby and Noah had been communicating with Leona and Kendall and got regular updates from

Anastasia about Hank's condition. They both talked about their life and how important their partnership was.

"Noah, darling, my honeybee, you know what you mean to me, right?"

"Of course, Abby, and you and Cassie are my world, and always will be the most important thing in my life. I will never take you for granite."

Susan was in the next room feeding the baby and she could overhear her daughter and Noah and it brought tears to her eyes that she could not hold back. They had so much of life ahead of them, and now with this new little one, they had no idea what was to come. She was happy to be a part of it all and wanted to ask them if she could stay here and help with little Cassie on a more permanent basis. But she wasn't sure how to approach it now with so much happening around them. She would just enjoy her time with the baby and do her best to comfort her daughter and son-in-law.

Susan laid the baby down to sleep for a bit and headed into the small kitchen of the townhouse.

"So, I was thinking about making a nice pot roast tonight and perhaps you could ask your friends to join us for dinner? I can run to the market for the last few items we need and will pick up a nice bottle of wine as well."

"Mom, that sounds wonderful. Maybe having my girls here and letting them spend some time with Cassie, we can take our minds off Hank for a few minutes. You are the best, Mom."

Noah could not contain himself. "Would you want to do this on a permanent basis Susan?" "I mean, live here, not just make pot roast."

"Yes, Abby chimed in. We have been discussing it and we could use your help. It has been so wonderful having you here. I know it is a lot to ask, but…."

Abby could not get the rest out before Susan jumped in and said "Yes!" "I mean, I have been thinking the same thing all week. I just love this little baby girl and I could help you out I think."

Noah and Abby hugged and smiled at Susan. "Come here", said Noah. "Group hug." The three of them hugged and Susan began to cry again. Abby felt a tear trickle down her face as well. They both looked at Noah and he grinned at them. "You big cry-babies, I love you both."

Back at the hospital Hank was out of surgery. The stent had been inserted and he was being moved into his room in the ICU. Anastasia was updated by the doctors and said she could see Hank in a couple of hours. With that, she headed to the hospital cafeteria for an early dinner.

Anastasia was surprised to see both Chad and Tucker sitting in the mostly empty café' talking quite seriously about something. She interrupted them with "why the heck are you boys still here?" Then she pulled out a chair and joined her friends. She updated them on Hank's condition and said they could see him in a few hours. She wasn't sure about anything else for now.

Tucker gave his sweet friend a hug and told her they were there for her if she needed anything. Chad, she noticed, seemed really tired and the dark circles beneath his eyes told the story.

"Chad, darling, you need to go home and get some sleep. Sorry honey, but you look worse than me."

After they all chatted for a bit, Chad agreed that he needed to leave and would come back up in the evening or perhaps in the morning. Tucker agreed to stay awhile to keep Anastasia company. She was hoping they could discuss the campaign and take her mind off Hank.

"Goodbye for now. I will update everyone else but do call us if there are any changes. And if you need anything, please reach out. Love you guys." Chad made his way out of the hospital, and it took a minute to figure out that he did not bring his car. He needed to call for a ride. Just then his phone rang, and it was Kendall.

"Hi honey, I am headed home. Do you need anything?"

"Um, I could use a ride home from the hospital", he told her.

"Okay, I am just around the corner. I will pick you up."

Chad was glad to see Kendall. He was so tired he just wanted to rest. But he could not sleep. He knew if he tried to nap at 3:00pm he would totally mess up his schedule.

Kendall arrived and explained how Abby and Noah invited them for dinner tonight. It was going to be casual, and Leona and Tucker were coming as well. Chad agreed it would be a good distraction from the day and he was starving for a good home-cooked meal.

He had learned recently that Susan was a great cook, so he was looking forward to the evening. The two decided to go home, take an hour nap, then shower and head to Abby's house.

Tucker stayed with Anastasia, and they did manage to talk a bit about the road ahead. She asked him about the news media frenzy, and he played it down so as not to worry her. But Anastasia was a wise one. She totally was not buying it. She knew she would have to do some damage control in the upcoming days and weeks. Her phone was loaded with calls and text messages from supporters, but also a few threatening comments telling her to just "get out of the race" and "be a good wife and stay home" kind of messages. This just lit a fire within Anastasia and made her more determined than ever to get back to work.

There was one message that gave her strength. It was from *Kathy Berry. Congresswoman Watkins – you have our prayers, our strength and our love. We are here for you, signed, The Gray-Haired Women.*

At around 6pm the nurse came out to get Anastasia so she could visit Hank. After some pleading, they agreed to let Tucker go with her. Hank was in a coma, and he would stay that way until the bleed was gone from his brain. Only time would tell how long it might take.

The pair sat with Hank silently for a few minutes. Then Anastasia began to speak to her beloved husband and tell him how she was there beside him. Tucker had never seen his friend speak so sweetly and gently to anyone in all their years of friendship. It was as if all the world went silent for a few moments. Tucker quietly removed himself from the room as Anastasia continued to cite sweet delicate tales from years past and talk about her needs for Hank to return to her.

Tucker had the hospital bring a hot meal to Anastasia and a beautiful bouquet of flowers with a note from him. "My dear friends, I will be here when you need me. I love you both and will keep you in my thoughts and prayers until Hank comes home. Tuck."

Tucker headed to Abby's to meet up with the rest of the group. He stopped and picked up a nice bottle of red wine and a nice bourbon to share with his friends. He was certain everyone would need a drink tonight.

CHAPTER SEVENTEEN

Mark Hunter was doing exactly what he had hoped to set out to do over a year ago. He managed to work his way into the campaign headquarters of the great Anastasia Watkins. He was learning all about her secret society of women that had been building her empire and he was sure he could work from within to destroy it all.

Mark had his own desires to be in the oval office but had settled recently on the next best thing. He was supporting his friend from Michigan, Governor Robert Jameson. Mark and Robert had attended college together and in recent years became very close friends. Robert had used Mark's connections in Real Estate to broaden his circle of supporters. Many promises had been made to bring Mark along with him on the campaign trail and eventually find him a spot in the Whitehouse. Mark Hunter had a lot of connections and was quite wealthy. Many of his customers in the antiques trade were also supporters of Jameson. Mark Hunter did not have what it would take to be a politician himself, not even a running mate for Jameson, but he was sure his friend would keep his promises to bring him along and find him a position in Washington…. Hopefully on the president's staff.

Leona seemed to have the right intuition about Mark and Mark knew it. He had managed to conceal his truth from Anastasia and the rest of the team, but he was having a more difficult time proving his allegiance to Leona. He hated Leona. She stood for everything he did not believe in. But, for him and his buddy Jameson to succeed, they had to take out Anastasia and that meant winning over Leona and Tucker Jackson and the rest of the tight-knit group of Watkins supporters.

While Mark was at campaign headquarters, he was working hard to leak information to reporters without being caught. He was also researching the contacts of the insider group of "Gray-Haired Ladies" as Leona called them. Who were these women, he thought. How in the hell did this bunch of women manage to build this underground empire that has suddenly exploded on the political scene.

Hunter had been working on Anastasia for a while and doing many things to gain her trust. He also was working Jameson the same way. He decided about eighteen months ago that Jameson was the way to get to the Whitehouse, but he knew his friend would need his help to knock out the biggest opponent, Anastasia Watkins. Governor Jameson had relied heavily on Mark Hunter over the past couple of years to help him get elected and he had agreed to pay him back. When the good Governor decided to run for President, he put together a contract with Mark to help him take out the Congresswoman and clear his path. There were financial incentives built in of course but the Governor knew Mark just needed the promise of power to string him along. So far, the plan has been working.

At the hospital the doctors were keeping a close eye on Hank and the blood clot was completely drained now. It only took about thirty hours to get there. Anastasia had not left her husband's side. Her friends brought her clothes and she showered at the hospital and slept in a rollaway bed next to her beloved. The group of friends kept things going at the office and at home. The dogs were fed, and they checked in on the house. Reporters finally got an update from Anastasia via a press release delivered by Leona.

"Hank Watkins is doing as the doctors had expected without any added concerns medically. His brain hemorrhaging has resolved, and he continues to rest currently. Watkins will be monitored for another 24 hours before he is awakened for further testing. Congresswoman Anastasia Watkins asks for your continued support and respect for her privacy at this time. She thanks everyone for the many well wishes she has received, and she looks forward to speaking to us as soon as she is able."

Abby spoke with Noah about their decision to bring her mother to DC to live with them and they decided to go ahead and begin looking for a larger home. The townhouse had been wonderful, but it was time to find a larger home to raise Cassie and share with Abby's mom. Perhaps their realtor friend, Mark Hunter, could help, thought Abby.

"Honey, what if we called Mark to help us find a home? I am sure he would be happy to help us."

Noah agreed and said he would stop by the campaign office this week and try to steal some time with Mark. He knew Mark had been busy helping Anastasia and the team, but he also was keeping his

Real Estate career going as well as his antique business. He was a busy guy, but he had been happy to pick up the slack whenever Anastasia needed anything, Noah was certain he would help him out.

Sandra James was busy making her own plans. She was thrilled to hear the kids were going to look for a larger place to live. She needed to get back to Alabama soon and tie up some loose ends there. She had not told Abby that she had a nice savings that she would gladly share with her daughter in exchange for a place to live in DC. But this was her plan. She hoped to give her daughter a nice financial gift that would allow them to make a substantial home purchase. She was glad to be able to do this and began to make her own plans for the future.

Back in San Francisco the group that called themselves "The Grays" for short, were working hard to keep the presidential campaign on track for their beloved Anastasia. The leader of the group was Amy Meadows. Amy had attended university with Anastasia, and they remained good friends through the years. Amy had followed her friends rise through the judicial system into the DA position in Georgia and they had met a few times over the years to discuss politics and how to create needed change for women in the world. Amy came from a conservative family that wanted nothing more than for their daughter to get married and raise children, but Amy had different ideas. She never married and she devoted her life to speaking out for women that had little or no voice. She was a champion for women getting equal pay and breaking through the glass ceiling of many organizations. Amy herself started a book publishing company that was now the leader in the industry. She has fought to keep many books on the shelves at US schools after so many were taken away in the late 2020's.

Amy and others in her group began to get threats via social media and Amy was recently approached in a convention of authors and told she should re-think supporting Watkins if she wanted to live. The threatening note was handed to her by someone in the crowd. She immediately involved authorities, but they could never determine the source. The FBI put Amy on the "high alert" list of people to watch. It didn't help calm her nerves but at least they knew of the threat.

Amy never said a word to Anastasia when this happened as she decided it was just a nutcase trying to scare her and she did not scare easily.

Today is a different story. As Amy was meeting with a small group of businesswomen a man wearing a black face covering burst into the office where some forty women were seated at a few scattered tables. The intruder raised an automatic weapon and began to fire into the air. He shouted out something about men control power and women need to step down, or something like that. Nobody could really tell what he was saying but the gunfire was rapid, and a light fixture fell from the ceiling crashing onto one of the tables below. The women scrambled beneath tables, and some ran towards the back doors to escape. The man aimed his gun at the crowd. *"Women with the gray hair should stop what they are doing. You cannot survive without us."* *"God will punish you if you do not stop."*

Just then, as the gunfire scattered around the room hitting furniture and walls, the security pounced on the armed man and tackled him to the floor. The shooter was stripped of his weapon as they carried him out of the room into the custody of the police that were racing into the building.

Amy and her colleagues were surveying the room, and it did not seem as though anyone had been shot or injured. The meeting room was a mess of broken glass from the fallen chandelier along with scattered bullet holes in the walls and furniture. Women were shuttering and crying and hugging one another fiercely. The police and ambulance had arrived, and everyone was checked out for any injuries.

Amy was relieved to know that no one was physically injured. They would all certainly have emotional scars for life, but she was thankful no one was shot or killed. It took at least an hour for the police to get statements from those in attendance and clear the room. Of course, the news media jumped on the story and were waiting outside the building to question the women as they left.

Amy gave the reporters what they wanted. She decided this was a perfect time to stand up for her cause and for her candidate while the world was listening.

"Hello everyone, I am Amy Meadows. I am the owner and CEO of Meadow Publishing. I am here today meeting with women from the area that support Congresswoman Anastasia Watkins for President of the United States. We came together to discuss how best to spread the word of the power that women have and how best to create a better world for women like us and our sisters. These radicals that come bursting into a room with a big gun are just cowards. They are nothing. They are afraid of losing something. But we are not here to take anything from anyone. And we are not scared. We are not afraid to stand up for what is just and fair for all people, including women of all ages, color and beliefs. The days of suppression are over. It is a new day. Watkins will show the world what the United States of America is all about. It is about our continued freedoms and our diversity. And most of all, it is about the women that make it all happen! We will no longer be silent and will NOT back down."

"I am happy to report there were no physical injuries here today to any of my friends and colleagues. Some stupid man with a warped ideology and illegal gun managed to shoot down a chandelier and some wallpaper. So good for him. Now he can go rot in hell as far as I am concerned, and I will continue to show women and girls everywhere that they are strong and powerful and to never be afraid. Thank you."

Reporters shouted their questions, but Amy ignored them and made her way to her car. She had a driver waiting for her and she scrambled into the back seat and asked him to please get out of here fast. She realized at that moment that she was shaking. Her heart was racing. She had a slight sweat bead trickling down her forehead. My gosh, she thought, I was

almost killed. Without thinking she said out loud
"what the fuck just happened?"

The driver asked her, "what is that ma'am?"

"Never mind, Thomas. Just take me home."

"Yes ma'am. Will do."

As they pulled up to the house there were more
reporters awaiting Amy. Since she lived in a gated
community, she wondered how they made it through
the front gates. I guess they have their ways, she
thought. "Thomas, will you please pull around back.
Then you can go. I won't be needing you any longer
today."

Amy went inside her lovely California ranch
home in the Bay area. Prominent businesspeople and
some Hollywood names were her neighbors. Her home
sprawled across some five acres of land, complete with
a large swimming pool and beautiful manicured
gardens. The house was small by her wealthy friends'
standards at only six thousand square feet of living
space. Amy loved the privacy and the proximity to her
office in the city. She lived here alone, with the
exception of three dogs, a cat and two birds. Her dogs
met her as usual at the front door with tails wagging.
The cat did not bother to move from her spot on the

large sofa where she had been planted for most of the day.

"Well, aren't you sweet boys. Hello Elvis. Hello Jack. Yes, I see you, Bob. Okay, let's get you your dinner. The dogs followed as usual and Amy kicked off her shoes, tried to shake the stress from her arms and opened the pantry door to scoop out the food. As the boys ate, Amy plopped down next to Sofie on the couch. "Well girl, how was your day?"

"Oh me? My day was great! Let's see…. There was a shooting by a masked man, but other than that it was pretty much business as usual."

Amy began to run through her mind all the events of the day. Then she tried to recall exactly what she said to reporters in her off-the-cuff delivery of a statement. She wondered if she was too irate. Was she too political. Did she look as scared as she was? It was all a lot to decipher, she thought, and she headed back to the kitchen. She decided a small pour of scotch over ice would help calm her nerves. Dinner could wait.

She flipped on the television to see her dear friend Anastasia, back in Washington, standing outside the hospital delivering a statement to the press. Oh, thank goodness it seems her dear friend's husband is going to make it. But her friend looked tired and sad. She was doing her best to say all the right things. And then she heard Anastasia refer to the shooting that had just happened in California. She was talking about her. Amy listened as Anastasia Watkins stood there and reiterated the words she had said earlier.

"My dear friend Amy Meadows was strong today. It is people like her that support me and give me my strength to continue forward on my journey. I thank you Amy and all the Grays out there that have stood by me the past few days and the past years. God bless you all. Now let's get on with it."

Wow, Amy could not believe it. After everything Anastasia was going through with Hank, she managed to thank her for her support. That is the kind of person she is, thought Amy. "She is good shit. God, I love that woman."

Back in DC the media was again all over this San Francisco shooting incident. And one reporter managed to find out about the threatening note and was trying to connect the dots to the shooter. The story of the threats against this presidential candidate were growing. There was a real concern for her life and the lives of the people that support her.

Mark Hunter was calling his friend Governor Jameson to discuss business. "We need to talk", was the message Mark left for his friend. Jameson called him back and was trying to assure him they were on the right course.

"Mark, my old buddy. How are you doing?"

"Well, I am hoping this idiot in San Fran doesn't cause us too many problems. Do you have any idea who he is Robert?"

"Of course not. But don't you worry. He did a fine job today and perhaps people will think about supporting such a radical stupid woman for president. This must help."

"I am not sure about that Bob. I mean Governor Jameson. Or should I call you Mr. President?" The two men laughed at their own stupid jokes. Each wasn't sure if the other was telling the truth about anything. Mark was concerned that Jameson was somehow involved in making this all happen, but he had no idea what to do about it.

"Well then, I will let you get back to it Sir. I have things under control at the Watkins campaign headquarters. It doesn't help that her husband is gaining sympathy support with his brain surgery. But I have some ideas that will help us down the road. Don't you worry. I got this."

Mark Hunter was not sure about anything lately. He was so sure of his path a few months ago, but then he started working on the campaign with the Watkins team, and something changed. For some reason that he cannot explain, he likes these crazy women. They are starting to get to him, he thought. And his friend Governor Jameson is sounding crazier every time they talk. It became clear to Mark that he had to figure out what he wanted from all this. Does he still want a place in the Whitehouse with Jameson and does he even trust Jameson to follow through as promised?

What if I do all this work just to have Bob move into the Whitehouse and leave me behind. It could happen, he thought. What if he keeps working for Watkins and she actually wins the election? His mind was racing with thoughts. It was a late night so he would think more about all this tomorrow. He thought it had been a good day in politics.

CHAPTER EIGHTEEN

The doctors briefed Anastasia on what to expect once they stopped the chemicals and Hank began to awake from his thirty-hour coma. Anastasia felt like she had not slept in days, and she just wanted to know Hank was going to wake up and come back to her. A number of problems could arise, and the doctors had a way of putting the worst case scenario out there, but Anastasia refused to consider any of those possibilities. Just get on with it, she thought.

After about 30 minutes her sweet man opened his eyes and said, "I am so hungry, is there food anywhere?" In that moment she knew all was going to bc just fine. She only worried about Hank when he was not hungry.

"Oh darling, there you are. It is about time you woke up and ate some dinner with me." She hugged Hank and a sense of relief came over her entire body. She breathed in a huge sigh. "I love you honey. I am glad you are back."

"Back from where", Hank said. "Who are you?"

Then he smiled that big toothy grin at her and said, "Sorry darling, I couldn't resist." Anastasia held up a fist and the doctor said, "please let's not punch anyone today" and the entire room broke out in laughter. Hank was so handsome; the nurses could barely contain themselves. With his head wrapped in bandages and tubes coming out of him he still managed to get the women's attention. Anastasia shook her head and smiled back at him. "He is all mine, ladies, so back off." They all laughed again.

The doctors gave all the details about what to do at home and what to watch for and decided that if Hank was doing fine tomorrow afternoon he could be discharged. Hank was thrilled at the thought of getting out of there. Anastasia wanted him home, but she wasn't so sure he was ready.

"Tomorrow?" "Isn't that a bit soon doctor?" "I want to be certain we are in the clear."

"Yes, unless anything unusual happens overnight tonight, he should be good to go tomorrow. Of course, he will be back in my office in a couple of days for a checkup."

Anastasia was so relieved that this was almost behind them. If she could hang on a few more days until Hank got the all clear from his doctors they could get back to some kind of normalcy. She stayed for hours talking to Hank and sent messages to their friends that he was awake and would be coming home tomorrow.

Kendall and Chad were so happy. Chad had a full day of rest, and he was back to his old self and ready to get back to work. Tucker and Leona got the message update as they were headed to the hospital. Anastasia had told the friends not to come. So, Leona and Tucker decided on dinner out tonight. They would linger over a nice meal and recall their time at the beach and begin to make their own plans for the future as Mr. and Mrs. Jackson. Tucker told Leona how much he loved her, and he was so glad to have her in his life.

"You know it is going to be a crazy few months ahead of us pretty lady. Promise me you will remind me to take a break and have a lovely dinner with you at least once a month if not more. I am going to need you to reign me in once Anastasia gets me out there on the campaign trail with her. Never forget that YOU are my girl."

"Oh, don't you worry Mr. Vice President, I will be right there by your side for this journey. YOU are my man, and don't you ever forget it."

The pair toasted to their present and future. They looked deeply into each other's eyes and finally Tucker said to his bride, "Can we get out of here now? I have a gift for you, but I must give it to you at home." He smiled his big smile and kissed her gently on the cheek as they left the restaurant. She grabbed his hand, and everything felt right in the world in this moment. She was expecting the *gift,* and she knew exactly what it was. She could not wait to get home.

Noah and Abby agreed that Sandra should make the trip back to Alabama now, while they were off work, and then she could return in a couple of weeks and stay for good. There was no house to sell or job to quit. Sandra James retired a couple of years ago and just did volunteer work at the local art gallery in town. But she did have to finish her plans and get ready to move to DC for the indefinite future. It was a big change, and she was nervous and excited at the same time. She thought about everything on the plane trip home. She was a grandma now and her daughter needed her. She did find DC exciting and full of things to explore so retirement there would be fun and interesting. And then there was the matter of her daughter and her friends working to elect the next president of the United States and it was going to be a woman! This was a lot to absorb. But Sandra always enjoyed a full life and loved adventure, so this was going to be great. She sat there looking out the plane window thinking of little Casandra Constantine that would grow up with strong women all around her and a woman president leading the charge. What a thought.

Leona could not sleep. She texted Abby and they exchanged several messages before picking up the phone to chat. They discussed Hank and Anastasia, the recent news coming out of San Francisco, and Mark Hunter. Leona still could not let it go.

"I just don't know what it is about that man. There is something too nice or too something. Am I nuts?"

"Well, I have never thought you were nut's Leona. You can be a bit eccentric at times. I was thinking of asking Mark to help us find a house in DC."

"Oh, that is great! I am excited for you. It will cost you a gazillion dollars, but you should go for it. I am sure he can help you."

"Didn't you say you were having dinner out tonight?" "How did it go?"

"Fantastic! Tucker is the best thing that ever happened to me girlfriend. I could not do this life without him. We had a wonderful evening, and he is passed out in the bed. I guess I was too much for him." The two friends laughed and finally called it a night. They were each glad tomorrow was the weekend. They all needed some rest. What a year it has been.

It was Saturday morning, and the doctors gave Hank the okay to escape home. Kendall and Leona and Abby all ran over to Anastasia's house and made sure it was ready for them. They tidied up and left a couple of nice casserole dishes in the freezer. Leona added a nice bouquet of fresh flowers on the kitchen island along with a bottle of champagne and a small little "welcome home" sign.   They fed the dogs and got out of there before the pair made it home.

At home, Hank and Anastasia were thrilled to be in their own space again. The dogs loved all over

Hank until Anastasia finally had to put them in the other room so he could have some peace. Hank insisted on staying up sitting on the couch. He said he could not imagine laying down in bed just now. "I have had enough laying in beds to last me a while, so I will just sit if that's okay."

After a while Hank said he had to see some of the news. He knew the friends and his wife had kept him from seeing anything on television or even looking at his phone for the last three days. He needed to reconnect with the world. He imagined there would be news of his operation and that was to be expected. He clicked on the set, and they sat down to watch CNN.

Anastasia put the set on pause. "Okay, there are a couple of things you need to hear from me." She went on to summarize the events in San Francisco and the media frenzy around recent threats against her campaign. Then she hit the un-pause button. It was just as expected. This was a campaign year after all and there was a lot happening out in the world. They watched for a bit then Hank said he had had enough and needed to rest. He laid down to rest and his wife laid by his side. They cuddled together and slept most of the day away. Hank was glad to be home with his love.

CHAPTER NINETEEN

Chad was at the Harley shop outside of DC that he helped manage. He had given up ownership of his shop in Atlanta when they moved to DC a few years ago. Since then, he has been happy to manage a small team of salespeople and the business has been doing well. In fact, the owner of the shop was retiring and asked Chad if he wanted to buy his franchise.

"Well, thanks Ted. That is a great offer, but I will need to think about it. I should probably talk it over with Kendall and get back to you. When do you need my decision?"

"If you can let me know by the end of the month that would be great. I need to notify corporate what I plan to do going forward. I just want to retire and go fishing and not think about this place anymore. Just let me know."

Chad would love to own this place, but that would mean a lot more time at work. He understands what is ahead of him and Kendall this coming year. He also wanted to approach his gal with the big wedding question. He needed to talk to Kendall tonight to sort out their future.

Kendall got home from the office and Chad was waiting with a hot pizza and a bottle of her favorite wine.

"What is all this?" "Oh no, is it something bad?"

"Would you not jump to conclusions lady. Can I not just fix dinner for you?"

"Um, dinner might be a stretch dear. The drive-through pizza pick-up place is pretty easy. But, hey, I am loving it! So, shoot. What is up?"

Chad began to explain about the offer to buy the Harley shop. He seemed excited about it and was putting a positive spin on his plan. Kendall could see how he wanted her to give him the okay to move forward.

"Sounds great to me!" "You should go for it if that is what you want to do."

Chad couldn't believe it. Was she really okay with all this? He explained how his savings from selling the other place in Atlanta was just sitting there and he could almost pay for the franchise without getting a loan. He was mostly concerned about the time it would take for him to get everything into his name and make some needed marketing changes to build up the business. But Kendall was really on board, and she was proud of Chad.

The pair finished up business talk and then Chad decided now or never for the big question.

"While I have your attention sweetie, there is one other thing we need to discuss."

"Oh no, I knew there was more. Bring it on."

Chad began to stumble on his words and was very nervous. He had not planned to do this now, but it just seemed like something he had to do.

"Kendall, honey, you know you are my world. I know this next year is going to be very busy for us both. I just need to know you will be here with me forever. I guess what I want to say is … Will you marry me?'

Kendall jumped up off the chair and into the arms of her lover. She had hoped he would ask her this question one day but had no idea it would be today. She could not stop smiling and then began kissing Chad and could not stop.

"Yes! A thousand times yes! I love you honey. I want so badly to be your wife." Kendall was shaking now and kept kissing Chad. "Come in the bedroom and let me show you just how much I mean it."

Chad began to pull off his shirt and climb out of his pants as fast as possible. Kendall had stripped off her dress and was already laying across the king size bed. Chad thought in that moment how lucky he was to have this beautiful creature as his own. She was striking, laying there, smiling, and reaching for him.

"Come here darling. Make love to your wife."

The lovemaking was wonderful and satisfying and the couple talked for hours about their future together. Chad would get the Harley shop he wanted, and Kendall would go on the campaign trail with her boss and help her get to the White House. It was about to be a crazy ride. And somewhere in there they would find time to have a wedding.

It was Sunday afternoon and the group of friends had plans to meet at Anastasia and Hanks for a quiet dinner. Hank was really wanting to see all his friends, so his wife indulged him. She made him agree to a short evening and he was to tell her at once if he felt light-headed or tired.

Abby and Noah were first to arrive with the baby in tow. This was their first venture out of the house with the baby. Kendall and Chad arrived next and for some reason, that Anastasia could not explain, there was something different about these two. Leona and Tucker finally arrived, and they brought the usual bottle of wine and some bourbon.

"Finally, just what I needed." Hank was smiling at his friends when Anastasia abruptly reminded him that he was on a no-alcohol diet for a few more weeks.

"Doctors orders dear."

"Fine. Just don't say I cannot have my ice cream or there will be trouble around this house."

All the friends caught one another up on their separate life events. Noah said he reached out to Mark to help find them a house in the city. Abbys mom had given the couple a fat check as her contribution, so they hoped to find a nice place with plenty of space for all of them. Everyone took turns holding little Cassie. They passed her around like a precious object that would crack at the wrong move. They talked about the future and Kendall could not hold it back any longer. She told her friends about the proposal during a toast.

Leona was raising her wine glass to say cheers to all her friends and to everyone's health…. when Kendall jumped in and said …. "To marriage! And to love! And to being Mrs. Chadwick Turner!"

The group erupted in "cheers!" The guys gave Chad the look. "When did all this come about dude?", said Hank.

"Actually, just a couple of days ago. It is just time. Oh, and I am buying the Harley shop too!"

"Well, now that is awesome. Here's to the Turners!"

It was a wonderful evening of sharing and laughs and the friends were anxious about the future. Lots of change was in the air. And quite a few angry politicians were out there making noise as well. There was a growing group of political opponents to the Watkins campaign, and they were stirring up fear and hatred that was unnecessary. Anastasia and Tucker shared a common goal to make it to the White House and put a stop to the craziness. This team of friends and colleagues would help them get there. But there would be a long road ahead of them.

The evening ended with everyone wishing Kendall and Chad the best and giving thanks that Hank was okay. All the women suddenly wanted their own baby and they decided they could babysit to get their needs met. There was a strong bond with this group of women, and it had made its way over to the men in their lives. The eight of them together were a force to be reckoned with and from any outsider looking in, it was a sight to behold. They were each fearsome in their own way but together they were a force. Each of them knew this. They could feel their power. They were stronger together and they knew it. They were unstoppable. And with the support around the country from the Gray-Haired Women's groups, there would be no stopping them. Destiny was theirs for the taking. They ended the night with handshakes and hugs all around and there was a feeling of great satisfaction and pride that encircled them as they left and went their separate ways home. Tomorrow was bound to be awesome.

Well, the next day was not awesome as expected. In fact, it was quite terrible. The news of Hank's operation and the shooting in California were already history. The media had moved on to new topics of discussion. There were now at least a dozen candidates in the run for the presidency. Leona was watching the news feeds and making her way to the office when her phone rang. It was Abby asking if she had seen the news. They could not believe that two of the Governor's running for president, had gotten together and put out a smear campaign against Anastasia.

"I guess they figured if they teamed up on her they could somehow win. Of course, only one of them can win so I don't quite understand why they are standing together as some kind of unified force to take the White House."

Leona agreed with Abby and told her she would look at all the recent news clips when she arrived at the office and would call her back to discuss their plans.

Abby had been at home six weeks now and was ready to get back to work. Now with this latest turn of events she was more than ready to get to the campaign headquarters. Her mother was expected back in town this week to stay with them permanently. She had released her apartment, sold most of her furniture and shipped a few items to Abby's house last week.

Noah had been in touch with Mark Hunter, and he was lining up some homes for the couple to tour. They hoped to go see a few houses this coming weekend. Susan would be back here, and she could watch Cassie for them.

Leona made it to the office and Mark was there, along with Kendall and Anastasia. "Looks like the team is here ready to hit the ground running", said Leona to the sad looking group.

Mark was first to say, "Oh, it is not as bad as it seems. Those guys are just scared to death of you ladies. They have to find something to use to gain some voters on their end."

Anastasia was visually upset. More like mad. She told herself there would be days like this and she had to keep her head high and push forward. "They are trying to say that my supporters in the Gray-Haired ladies' groups are some kind of mafia. They are trying to link them to the shooter in California and actually said he was planted as a media gimmick." She had more words to say, and the group tried to calm her down and make some plans for rebuttal.

Leona had already been working on some things and they had put together a nice positive campaign ad. Kendall was helping finish it up and they were releasing it this week. It was finally time to begin real campaigning. The team worked to schedule stops in California, Arizona and Washington state. From there they would travel by train across the Midwest and fly home from Chicago. There were a few other stops later in the month on the East coast. It was about to be a busy month.

Mark managed to slip out and told the team he had some real estate business to deal with today. In fact, he needed to touch base with the two Governors from California and Michigan that had just published the smear campaign. Much of the information they had used was provided by Mark Hunter. He had continued to get insider information during calls and meetings and was privy to most of the correspondence coming and going out of the Watkins headquarters. The team trusted Mark. He was getting paid handsomely by the Governors for his work.

"Governor Jameson, nice to talk to you Sir."

On the call was also the California Governor and a couple of other campaign managers working the other side of the race. It seemed like the old days of a two-party system, but Mark knew otherwise. He just had to play the game.

Robert Jameson was the mastermind behind the nasty advertisements slamming Anastasia and her Gray ladies. He was now on this call and was saying they were a "bunch of old ladies with no real power or good sense", and Mark knew he was dead wrong.

"Gentlemen, if I could just offer a word here. I think you are underestimating this group and the candidate. They are quite powerful, and the reach is far and wide. You will need more than some ugly adds to win this one." As Mark was talking there was much grumbling on the call. Mark listened to the comments and what he thought was a fair amount of bullshit before ending the call.

Mark Hunter was what one would call a real "go-getter" kind of guy. He knew a lot of people and he had been quite successful in his real estate career. He also managed to build a large network of influential people in the antiques circle in DC. But finding purpose in his life had been a struggle. Most of the family in Mark's life had lost touch with him. He moved several times over the last few years before settling in DC. One of his antique connections introduced Mark to Governor Jameson. They had become fast friends and Mark usually called his friend "Bob" when it was just the two of them.

Robert Jameson was hungry for power. He and Mark had that in comment. This is where their story began and together, they believed they could somehow make their way together into the White House. Bob had the political connections and Mark had the money connections. Mark hosted a few parties last year and invited the Governor as a prominent guest speaker.

But recently, Mark had begun to examine his life and question what it was he liked about Robert Jameson. He was finding it more difficult to answer that question. And the more time Mark spent with Anastasia Watkins and the entire Watkins team, the more Mark was drawn into their circle of kindness and integrity. As the team trusted Mark more and more, there were plenty of opportunities to steal information and share it with Jameson. But, for reasons unknown to Mark, he was finding it harder to do so.

These people trust me, he thought. And they treat me as a friend. They are good people. Mark began to question everything about his life and the path he was on. But he had taken quite a bit of money from the good Governor and in exchange for that he owed him information.

Mark came back to the Watkins campaign office after closing hours. It was near eight o'clock and the place was quiet. Mark let himself inside the building with his key. He began to cipher through meeting notes from the day. Then he came across the list of leaders of the Gray-Haired Ladies groups. He had never seen this before. Of course, it was locked in Anastasia's desk, which Mark had pried open. With the list in hand, Mark continued to look through notebooks and file folders looking for anything he could provide to Jameson.

Suddenly the door popped open and there stood Leona. She had returned for some paperwork she wanted to read over tonight at home.

"What the hell are you doing here Mark?"

"Oh, I uh, was looking for some notes I made earlier and I just …. Well, what are you doing here?"

The exchange was awkward at best. Leona was sure she had finally caught him red-handed. She never trusted this guy like Anastasia did. Now she had him where she wanted him.

"I think you should sit down, and we should call Anastasia to get her over here."

"Now that is not necessary. Hold on there. I wasn't taking anything. I just needed my notebook."

"So, is that it? That looks like something else. Show me what you have in your hand Mark. Do it!"

"Okay, fine. Here."

"Oh my God. I knew you were a creep. What did you plan to do with this? Who are you working for?"

"No one. I just wanted more information about these so-called *Gray Ladies* so I could understand who they were and how they operated." "That is all, I swear."

"Well, I don't believe a word you are saying, but let's just pretend you are telling the truth. Now what?"

Mark began to break down. Leona thought he was about to cry. He was nervous. He tried to explain how he had gotten tied into working for Jameson and how he wanted nothing better than to get himself out of that mess.

Leona listened for an hour while Mark went into detail about everything. Then he begged for her forgiveness and asked her not to tell Anastasia. He wanted to stay on her team. He would do anything she wanted if he would just have a chance to clear his name and help get Anastasia elected.

Leona could not believe all of this. Now Tucker was calling and looking for her. She was due back home a while ago. She made excuses about getting into something at work and she was on her way in a few minutes. Leona was trying to absorb all of this and decide what to do with this guy.

"So here is the deal. I know I should turn you over to the authorities and let them have their way with you. I am not sure what, besides theft of information, you might be charged with, but you could be in big trouble with Jameson for sure. But then, I am wondering how you might work for our team and help us take Jameson down. Does that appeal to you?"

"It sure does. I would love nothing more than to see that slimebag get what he deserves. And he certainly does not deserve to be president. How can I help?'

Leona wasn't sure if she was doing the right thing here but agreed to let Mark leave. "I own you now Mark. You and I will meet tomorrow and figure all this out."

"Okay, I get it. I will see you tomorrow for sure. And thanks for believing in me. I promise to fix all this."

At home Leona was telling Tucker what had just happened. The thing most important to Leona and her friends and especially her husband, was honesty. They shared everything and no one in their group had secrets. Especially when it came to work and family.

So, Leona told Tucker everything and did her best to keep him from running directly to the police. He wanted nothing less than to see Mark Hunter locked up. But after talking it over and going through every scenario, they decided to bring it to the group for a decision. It was now close to midnight, but this could not wait. Tucker called Anastasia. She was not asleep, but Hank was.

"What the heck is up Tuck? It is late, so this must be important. Spill the beans."

He explained all the details of Leona's encounter with Mark earlier that evening and how they left everything. Tucker still wanted to call the authorities, but Anastasia wanted to talk with him first. She needed more answers about who hired him to do what and how she could use this information. She thanked them for the call, and she texted Mark to meet her at her office at 6:00am.

"Mark, it is Anastasia. I know everything. Be at my office at 6:00am sharp tomorrow. Let's chat."

Mark knew things were going to get ugly, but he also had come to understand that Anastasia and her friends were savvy and much smarter than Jameson. Mark wanted to make this right with Anastasia. He hoped it was not too late to switch teams and keep himself out of jail.

Leona called Abby and Kendall and explained it all and told them to wait until Anastasia met with Mark before doing anything. "Don't call anyone. Sit on this until morning and we will all meet at the office and figure it out."

Morning came and Mark was waiting outside the office door for Anastasia. She arrived with Tucker promptly at 6:00am. "Come inside. Let's talk."

Mark explained how he had gotten mixed up with Robert Jameson and how that all snowballed into doing his dirty work. He told Anastasia he had such respect for her and what she stood for, and how he wanted out of his situation with Jameson, but he just couldn't figure out what to do to end it. He had been trying but he had taken a good sum of money from the Governor, and he owed him something in return.

Tucker wanted so badly to just punch Mark square in the face. "How dare you bring all this crap to our laps. We trusted you. Anastasia relied on you, and you used her for your stupid financial gain. What a low life you are, Mark. But this is not my call. The boss will decide your fate, so I suggest you throw yourself at her mercy."

Anastasia suggested that if Mark really wanted to do the right thing, then he should be given the chance to do so. She suggested that Mark be able to get himself out of the deal with Jameson. He could not provide any valuable information to help with his smear campaign against her, but perhaps he could provide false information that would backfire on Jameson.

After a couple of hours, they had come to an agreement. About that time the rest of the team showed up with coffee and angry faces, ready for battle.

"Ladies, before anyone sets up the guillotine, you should know we have come to an understanding with our fellow traitor." Anastasia brought the team together in her private office, while Mark sat in the next room with Tucker, just hoping to stay alive.

They all agreed with the plan. Mark would be given the opportunity to prove himself to her team. He would provide just enough wrong information to Jameson and his possie to cause a media nightmare for the opposition. Then Mark would give back the money he was fronted by Jameson. It was just sitting in his account. Mark admitted he had refused to spend a dime of it for fear of what may happen down the road. His instincts had proved to be correct.

Several days went by and it was business as usual on the Watkins campaign and Anastasia, along with Tucker, Leona and Kendall, were hitting the campaign trail. Abby had plans to join them in Chicago. Mark was left to do his dirty work and get out of the Jameson nightmare he had created for himself.

Noah and Abby were set to see some houses with Mark but considering everything that had happened they decided to use a different realtor. Abby's mom, Susan, was back in town and getting settled. She would be caring for Cassie today while the couple toured three homes they may want to purchase. They had viewed about a hundred properties online and narrowed the list to three. They hoped to decide this weekend.

The realtor showed the properties to Abby and Noah, and it was the last of the three homes that seemed to be the one for them. It had a finished basement with a full bedroom, bathroom and kitchen, so Susan could have her own space. Downstairs walked out to a patio and beautiful koi pond surrounded by a landscaped fenced yard and inground pool. Abby was not looking for a pool, but once they saw this house, it was perfect for them. Noah loved the kitchen and the hardwood floors. The home was older, and it had some character with arched doorways and thick crown molding. There was even a three-car garage, and the house was within walking distance of a school. Abby thought it could not be more perfect for them. The price was a little above what they initially wanted to pay, but with the added money from Susan, they could make it work.

Chad was busy getting his franchise Harly shop set up to work the way he wanted it to work. The prior owner did an okay job of things, but Chad had some ideas he wanted to implement right away to increase sales. He gave his love some extra hugs and kisses before she departed for three weeks on the campaign trail. They both had work to do and decided they would talk about wedding plans next month.

Anastasia did not want to leave Hank and she tried to talk him into going with them on the campaign trail, but Hank had other plans. He had missed a few weeks of work and needed to get back into the swing of things at his office.

Hank mostly worked from home and traveled to meet with clients. He was a financial advisor with a big international firm, and because of his tenure and expertise, they allowed Hank to basically make his own schedule. He had several clients he had worked with for many years, and he managed their portfolios. He decided after some discussion with Anastasia, that he should begin to pull back from the job so he could spend more time with her. She would need him by her side as the election got closer. It was not fair to his clients to give them only minimal attention. He had been relying heavily on his partners to help him out the past few weeks since his accident. It was time to make some changes.

Hank made a few trips to visit in person with his clients and explained he was moving their portfolio to his partners. They all understood. Most of Hank's clients were thrilled to collaborate with him and they loved his wife, so it made sense that he supported her and would get her to the White House!

It was a long couple of weeks and Hank was tired. He felt as though he had fully recovered from his surgery, but he knew he had been pushing things. His doctors had told him he would not feel 100% for at least a month or longer. So, he was trying to be patient. He worked on getting work in order and then he called Chad and Noah and suggested a day of golf.

Chad was happy to set a day for golf if they were not getting on a plane to Florida. He still had some shellshock from that ordeal. He had not played golf since that time and thought it was a good idea.

Noah was also glad to meet up with the guys while all the girls were out of town. He had been so busy with the baby, the new house stuff and his mother-in-law, he was happy to get out for the day. So, they set the date to meet up Friday for eighteen holes.

Mark called Chad on Thursday to catch up and see how things were going with their realtor. He said he felt really bad about everything and wanted to make it up to him. Chad was still fuming about Mark and all his bullshit but realized they could use a fourth person tomorrow to round out the game. "Would you want to join the guys for a foursome tomorrow?" "We could use an extra player and maybe someone to carry our bags and buy the beer."

"I would love that man. I owe you all so much.
I really want to do right by you guys. I am in. That is,
if the other guys will be okay with it. Do you think it is
okay?"

"It is fine Mark. We are all adults, and these
guys are cool. They do hate you right now, but we
need a fourth, so it is all good. Bring your beer
money."

Mark was thrilled to get the invite. He had been
working on some things with Jameson. He sent back
his money. He said he didn't need to be paid for any
services. Jameson didn't really care and never thought
twice about it. He just kept prodding Mark for more
information on the Watkins campaign that he could use
against her. Jameson was losing patience with Mark
and insisted on something he could use. So, Mark put
together a totally false bunch of information about the
Watkins party and the Gray-Haired Ladies that wasn't
really a thing. He told the Governor he should go out
there and call it all fake news. There was no such
thing, and the Gray-Haired Ladies were a fabrication
by Watkins. "It is all made up Sir. Have you seen any
proof of anything? Of course not, because it is fake.
Watkins and her team are pretending to have all this
support, but they really do not. You should call them
on it."

CHAPTER TWENTY

Out on the campaign trail the friends were having the time of their lives. Anastasia was amazing at rallies and town hall meetings. She spoke with enthusiasm and honesty. She had a way about her that showed strength and courage. The team had hired a stylist to bring the right clothes and do her hair and makeup, but Anastasia fought them every day. She wanted to be natural. "I am who I am", she would say. But the ladies surrounding her kept her on track.

"Honey, we just want you to be the best YOU possible. We need you to look good on screen, you know. So just let them do their job, then go out there and be fabulous."

Kendall and Leona struggled to keep Anastasia looking great and sounding great every single day. They had managed to get her to cut her long straight hair into a bob length. She refused to color the gray. "It is my statement."

"Gray ladies unite! We are getting older but better!" The friends all agreed, and the crowds adored this lady. Something about her made you listen to what she had to say. This is how they had all ended up here on the campaign trail with her. People would shout out questions and Anastasia would pause, look them straight in the eye, and give her best answer.

Anastasia was on a roll and other candidates out there were struggling. Robert Jameson, Governor of Michigan, was the only one that had managed to build a following. He was very conservative and had a way of talking to the men in the crowd. He was known to say things about how women just weren't cut out for politics and needed to let men do "men's work", or something like this. It crawled under Anastasia's skin for sure.

It was the last stop in Chicago before the exhausted team would do a last town hall and then get on the plane to head back to DC. They had been to six major cities and done no less than a dozen town hall meetings. They were a little tired, but the crowds were growing, and this kept them all energized. Also, they were looking forward to finally having Abby on the trail with them. She was waiting for them at the hotel in downtown Chicago.

"Abby! Finally, you are here. We missed you!"

Abby had arrived the day before and had a nice dinner planned at the hotel that evening. The group met at the restaurant in a quiet private room in the back. The food and wine were wonderful, and the stories were plenty!

Abby had to bring them up to date on her mom moving back, finding the perfect house, and Cassie keeping her up all night. She was more than ready to be here getting all the campaign updates. The women talked into the late evening about all the work they had done and what was left to do. They could once again feel their power as a team. They all brought energy and trustworthiness to the table.

There was going to be a rally in the park tomorrow in Chicago before they left for home. Everything was arranged and Abby had set up several keynote speakers to introduce Anastasia. They were expecting a huge crowd. The team of friends decided to call it a night so they could get some needed rest before tomorrow.

It all went as planned. The crowds began to gather around 2:00pm for the speakers that would start at 4:00pm, then Anastasia would take the stage at 5:00pm. It was a perfect Saturday in September, and the weather was nice outside. The sun was shining, and everyone was happy.

After several keynote speakers were done the crowds began to roar for their candidate for president. Signs were waving in the crowd and flags were flying. There was even a flyover of bomber planes just before the candidate took to the stage. There was a rush of adrenaline in Anastasia's veins. She looked at her friends standing next to her on the back side of the stage and smiled her big toothy smile.

"I love you girls. Thank you for being here." With that she ran onto the stage and the crowd roared. She smiled and waved at the people in front of her. These were her people. They supported her and what she believed in. She wanted nothing more than to give them her absolute best self.

"Hello Chicago! I am Anastasia Watkins, your next President of the United States!" "I love you Chicago!"

The next morning the ladies were moving slowly towards the airport and their return home. They met for a quick breakfast and over coffee they summed up the prior evening to a success. What a way to end a trip, thought Anastasia. "Who is ready to go home?", she asked.

Just then the television in the hotel lobby had CNN on with a scrolling banner of "Breaking News" from the Jameson campaign. Reporters were discussing how Governor Jameson gave a speech last evening and told the crowd in the room that Watkins was a liar. Everything her campaign has said about the support from the "so-called Gray-Haired Ladies, is all made up" and there is "no such group" out there. Reporters were surrounding Jameson as he spewed out untruths and more fabrications. He was on a roll, that was certain.

Anastasia could not believe her ears. Kendall and Leona were smiling. They all knew this was the work of Mark Hunter. Abby said, "He did it, didn't he." They were all in a state of shock. What would happen now? Then all their phones began to ring. Calls and texts were flowing and suddenly the hotel was filled with reporters swarming Anastasia and her team.

"Congresswoman Watkins, is any of this true?"

"What is your response to Governor Jameson?"

"Please, can you tell us about the made-up supporters you call the Gray-Haired Ladies? Was it all a lie?"

Anastasia motioned to her team, and they all stood up and left the table and headed to their car without comment.

By the time the plane landed it seemed like the whole world was questioning whether Anastasia Watkins was telling the truth about anything. All her supporters were wondering what was true and what was not.

Then, it became clear. Women around the country were marching in the streets. The Gray-Haired Women's Society was out in full force. They were yelling from street corners, cafés and church pulpits. Reporters could not cover every story but managed to find enough to smother CNN and every other news station with testimonials about the women that have supported Anastasia Watkins and continue to support Anastasia Watkins for president! It was a firestorm of media stories that made the poor Governor Jameson look like a fool.

Thousands of people took to the streets of Washington, Manhattan, Newark, San Francisco, Los Angeles, Baton Rouge, Kansas City, Louisville, Nashville, Detroit, Columbia, Phoenix, and every other city in the US!

It was like nothing anyone has seen before in history. This Governor just made the biggest mistake of his life. He dared to say that this woman that was running for president was not telling the truth and that she had no real supporters. Well, he was wrong. She had plenty. She had more than plenty. She was well on her way to the White House in a few months and it did not seem as though there would be any stopping her.

The team headed home from their trip and Anastasia was met with a crowd outside of her home in DC and people lined the streets of her neighborhood. She managed to make it inside and was met by Tucker and Hank. They just stood there smiling. Soon after, the rest of the group arrived at her house. "We couldn't go home. We had to be here with you in this moment", said Abby.

"Holy Crap!", said Leona. "I mean, wow!"

"I know, right", said Kendall.

They all sat there in disbelief. They turned on the news and watched as the people spoke.

"We are not made up. We are real. We are the Secret Society of Gray-Haired Women, and we are a secret no more!"

"Watkins for president!"

"She is our leader, and you will not stop us now!"

Reporters stayed for a couple of hours then began to leave when they realized Anastasia was not making a statement. She did send out Tucker to address the crowd and he asked them to kindly disperse for the evening.

"Your candidate is more than thrilled at this outpouring of support. We just returned from a long campaign tour and Anastasia will be speaking to you tomorrow. Thank you for your support. We love you all. Good night!"

It seemed they were well on their way to the White House. The rest of the campaign should be interesting, thought the group of tired travelers.

Abby headed home to see her baby girl and get some rest as tomorrow would be a big day. She also had a house to close on in the coming weeks. There was no time to discuss any of this tonight.

Kendall was excited to see Chad and their sweet puppy Joe. Her guys had missed her, and she missed them. They had a lot to catch up on with the new business venture. She was sure Chad would be talking about his store all night.

Leona and Tucker hung around for dinner with Anastasia and Hank. The guys talked about golf and the friends were deciding what to do with Mark Hunter. It seemed he had pulled off something pretty spectacular after all. Leona decided she might just like this guy.

CHAPTER TWENTY-ONE

What a few weeks it had been. After a few days of rest the Watkins campaign was back at it. Other rival candidates were dropping from the presidential race every day. Jameson had lost most of his support when he tried and failed to take down Anastasia Watkins. And he had been a fool to suggest the Gray-Haired Women were a fabrication. That was far from the truth.

Mark Hunter had been busy doing his best to remove himself from any connections to the Michigan Governor. He truly was working for Watkins now and had proven he was loyal to her campaign. Even Leona had come around and decided to give him a second chance. He did pull off an amazing stunt by feeding misinformation to Jameson. And Jameson could not publicly condemn Hunter because of his connections with him in the past.

The California Governor was still doing his best to stay in the race, and this suddenly seemed to be the most troubling opponent for Anastasia. There was no two-party system anymore, but that didn't keep the general public from swaying as more Republican or more Democratic with opposing views on hot issues.

The environment was a big issue and had been for the last few elections. The US was the world leader in making corrections to our eco systems including waterways, natural gas and other ways to save the planet. Everything was recycled these days and the state of California had led that charge. Anastasia supported the Governor in many of his prior bills before Congress. She was finding it difficult to condemn him but managed to find some differences that stood out that she could use in her campaign.

California government was shaky, at best. While they had proven leadership in the environmental tasks, there were crime issues in the state and immigration problems at their borders. The local government pushed away federal funding and aid but now they were falling flat, and Anastasia was quick to show the Governor failed his people by not working with Washington these past few years. Several key factors helped Watkins keep a slight margin ahead of the Governor in the recent polls.

One of the things Anastasia was most proud of was her bill that passed into law prior to the previous election. She and a group of other congressional leaders managed to turn the voting system on its end. There were no longer polling locations and ballots inserted into machines. An *App* had been created for each person to place their votes via their cell phones, laptops or home computer. For those voters without such technology, they could stop at a local library or police station to vote at a kiosk.

This had been the greatest invention of the era as far as most voters were concerned. All the prior years of allegations of voter fraud were erased. An independent technology company housed in the FBI headquarters ran the logistics and counted the votes. The system was assessed several years prior to being pushed out to the public. The prior election and all local elections have been smooth sailing for the last eight years.

The time had finally come for a woman to be president. This seemed like a reality now and the team just needed to keep Anastasia as the frontrunner.

Tucker had become more visible and was doing more town hall meetings around the country. Tucker was an excellent speaker and his finance background made speaking to business owners and CEOs come with ease. He provided a softer edge to Anastasia's no-nonsense way of addressing a crowd. Tucker had a real way with people. And he was tall, dark and handsome which had most women eating out of his hand. Leona collaborated with her stylist to help dress Tucker for events. He mostly wore tailored suits but left off the usual necktie and went for a sportier look.

Tucker and Anastasia made a great team. They were a nice balance of knowledge, understanding and honesty. The pair had toured Europe and Anastasia had met many world leaders during her time in Congress. Tucker had done business with the Chinese and Korean governments and while the US had enforced thousands of sanctions for the sake of world peace and US prosperity, the communications had been good, and this pair were welcomed as world leaders. It seemed they were unstoppable.

All was going well, then on a recent trip down the eastern coast the unimaginable happened. Both Anastasia and Tucker, along with Hank and Leona, as well as Abby and Kendall, were all on board the *Silver Bullet Train* headed from North Carolina to Miami, when the train was abruptly stopped on the tracks. This new high-speed train had just been making this trip for the past year and there had not been a single issue. The train would run non-stop at a speed of 120 mph and a trip that would normally take 12 hours would just take 6 hours. It was a great invention, and many travelers would prefer this in lieu of flying or driving. This was one of six new *Bullet* trains running in the US.

This train not only had the occupants of the Watkins campaign team but there were another hundred bodies on board, all paying a premium to be traveling with this group. Security was on high alert, and everything seemed to be going well until the train reached the border of Florida. Watkins and her group were not aware that the Michigan Governor was holding a huge rally in Jacksonville Florida the day the train was to pass through the city. For several days leading up to this, there was talk about Jameson's campaign stirring up trouble for the Watkins campaign. Jameson had been speaking early in the day and was going on a rampage about Watkins and how she was this wealthy Congresswoman that could use voters' money to pay for her premium ride on the Bullet Train. This politician also told some other lies about Anastasia and said she was having an affair with Tucker. Of course, none of this was the truth, but it managed to rile up a large group of Jameson supporters that now gathered around the train station.

The high-speed trains traveled on a rail system that was built some 30 feet above ground. This allowed for other traffic to travel beneath the railway. There were stations where the train could stop if it needed to, but most trips were non-stop, as this one was.

The Jacksonville crowd became more and more angered by the Jameson speech and when they realized the train was going to pass by a large group made its way to the train station and rode the elevators to the platform next to the rails. The police were there in force and some rioters were hauled off. The police were notifying the Watkins security detail and the train conductors they had a problem at the station. Just then as the train began to slow down, a large crowd hoisting *Jameson for President* signs, ran onto the rails and across the tracks, hanging from railings and shouting out unrecognizable chants. Items were tossed onto the tracks and the conductor was doing his best to slow the high-speed train to a stop. The brakes were screeching and horns bellowing, and it appeared some people would be struck by the train. Just then the train came to a halt as the passengers inside were tossed around.

Anastasia and Hank were thrown to the floor. Hank fell and his head hit a steel handle causing him to be knocked unconscious briefly. Everyone on the train screamed loudly. Alarms bells were ringing. Messages that no one could decipher were being dispatched over the speaker system.

"Stay in your seat with safety belts fastened."

"Emergency stop ahead."

"Do not exit the train. Stay in your seat until the security alarms stop."

"Tucker, what is happening?", Yelled Leona. She was looking around for her friends. Anastasia was on the ground next to Hank. There was blood on the floor. "Oh my God, his head. Hank needs attention. Help!"

Abby was in the next car and had been meeting with some reporters. They had all been tossed around like rag dolls and several of them were bleeding from cuts on their arms and heads. The luggage had fallen from overhead bins and had struck several reporters in the head. The train security crew were quickly picking up passengers and luggage from the floor.

Finally, the conductor came on the intercom system to give an update on their status. The track had been cleared and they would be departing unless anyone on board was declared to have a medical emergency. The train would leave in five minutes. An EMT on board was checking each passenger for injuries.

Outside the train the crowds were still angry. A few of the rioters were injured when they fell from the railings onto the tracks. The train did not strike anyone. The police were removing the people from the platform. The reporters had followed the crowd and were reporting live on CNN.

Anastasia refused to leave until she was certain everyone outside the train was safe. Against security concerns she stepped outside the train. She yelled to the crowd that she was sorry they had to depart. She hoped everyone was okay and it was not her intention to have anyone injured, EVER! Then, without warning, the train began to depart again, and security grabbed Anastasia and pulled her back inside the train.

"You crazy women." Said one of the security officers. "Get inside and away from those nuts."

"They are not nuts." Anastasia said with a smile.

"They are enthusiastic, like the rest of us. And they want to be heard."

Kendall and Abby grabbed Anastasia and hugged her. "Are you okay honey?" Then Hank popped up with his hand holding a bloody rag to his forehead. "Well, that was something, now, wasn't it?"

Anastasia looked around to survey the damage. She wondered at this moment if it was all worth it. What is wrong with people, she thought. One minute I think I am on the right track and then suddenly the world is turned upside down and I am not sure what I am doing.

"Hank, are you okay honey?" She looked at her love and could not believe that Hank, of all people, suffered a head injury during this trip. "Your poor head." She looked into his eyes. Hank looked back and he said to her, "babe, this is just a little bump in the road, don't you worry, I have a really hard head. I will be fine. Just maybe get me a brandy." With that, the group of friends laughed aloud. "Me too!", Said Tucker. "And me!", Said Leona. Then Anastasia said she needed to check out the rest of the passengers on the train. Her security detail led the way, and Anastasia made her way into the other train cars to talk with the passengers.

Everyone was in shock to see the presidential candidate standing there in front of them. It appeared that most everyone was okay besides a few bumps and bruises. Anastasia had quite a group gathered around as she said how sorry she was that this had happened. She was visibly upset, and the other passengers could tell from the strain in her voice. There was a comforting type of calm that Anastasia emitted as she spoke to the group. They listened to her every word and gave her a standing ovation at the end of her speech.

It was not a speech though, and the crowd knew it. It was a sincere apology for their trouble and inconvenience. She thanked them all for their understanding. She hoped that everyone was okay, and that tomorrow would be a better day for each of them. Many in the group wanted photos with the Senator and they asked for her autograph. Each person in that train car knew at that moment that they were in the presence of something or someone spectacular. There was no denying that this lady was special. Most of the crowd was certain this was their next US President.

The train arrived in Miami and the station erupted with crowds and reporters waiting to hear from the passengers and the Watkins campaign team. Before exiting the train, a group of physicians boarded the train and checked out everyone with any kind of injury. Anastasia insisted that every single passenger and worker on board the train be examined. She agreed to cover the expenses.

Hank was checked out and given the okay. He had superficial cuts and nothing of concern. Kendall sprained her wrist from falling when the train stopped suddenly. Everyone else seemed to check out just fine. This was just another one of those crazy campaign stories.

The group met in the Miami stadium for the planned rally that evening. Hank stayed at the hotel to get some rest. It was a successful event without any issues. The news media was all over the Jacksonville train mishap and all fingers were pointing to Governor Jameson as the leader of the pack that caused the chaos. His constituents were getting more out of control, but at the same time they were dropping in numbers. The polls showed fewer followers in the Jameson campaign. The California Governor was also losing steam and Congresswoman Watkins was building momentum.

More rallies were happening nationwide led by the Gray-Haired Women groups. It was now only a couple of weeks until election day. The team would be wrapping up the cross-country tours and rallies and there was just one final debate that would take place in Washington next week, just a week ahead of voting day.

Currently there were just four candidates on the ballot that had made it to the election day finish line. The two Governor's from Michigan and California, and one businessman from Florida. The businessman, Jesse Stone, had worked alongside NASA and was heavily invested in the new space station where it was said the US would begin to build housing soon. Yes, a group of wealthy business owners had put together and gotten approval to build space homes that would dock onto the current space station. It was a concept that was extremely exciting for the public and it was helping Jesse Stone work his way towards the presidency. The only problem for Jesse was his moral values. He had several run-ins over the years with the legal system and had been caught spending thousands of dollars on prostitutes, both male and female. He had fathered a couple of children and treated the women badly and the press had a field day with all of it. Team Watkins was certain he would not be a player on election day.

CHAPTER TWENTY-TWO

Washington DC was buzzing with election day approaching. Anastasia and Tucker had blown it out of the water with the recent rallies and town hall meetings. The debate had gone as expected and Anastasia was in charge, taking on questions and giving intelligent answers that the public could understand.   She and her team felt good about election day.

Abby and Noah got news that the home they were bidding on was to be theirs! It was perfect for them, and their growing family and the lower level worked great for Abby's mother, who was now their official grandma/nanny. They would be closing in thirty days, so they needed to get packed. Their townhouse had sold fast and was in escrow to close in 45 days. Timing worked out on both sides. Mark Hunter had stayed out of the deal but in recent weeks he had helped with getting the dates all lined up. Mark knew the realtors on both sides of the buy and sell deal and he was glad to help his friends.

Chad and Kendall set a wedding date. They decided to wait until after the inaugural day events. They were certain their friend would be the new president and that took precedent over their wedding plans. They tentatively set aside a few dates in April and May for consideration.

Leona was wrapping up her day and her phone rang.

"Hello, Watkins for President! May I help you?"

"This is Genevive Walker, from Catholic Adoption Services, I am looking for Leona Jackson."

"That is me. I mean I am she…you are who?"

"Leona, may I call you Leona?"

"Yes, that is fine."

"You have been on the waiting list for adoption for over a year now. I see you have been very patient. But

I am calling to give you some news. We have a baby for you."

"Baby? I mean, baby!!" Leona was about to scream. After all the approvals and meetings several months ago, it had been silence from the agency, with the exception of a few emails and other correspondence, that all said to be patient.

"Okay, by having a baby for me…you mean you actually have a baby for me to adopt? Like now?"

"That is exactly what I am saying ma'am. The child was just born today. It has been assigned to you and Mr. Jackson and after paperwork is completed and the necessary health checks are complete you can take him home in a few days."

"Um, okay! Oh my gosh. I can't believe this day has arrived. And just in time for the election!"

"Excuse me, the election?"

"Oh, yes, I am sorry. I work for the Watkins campaign for president. I have been terribly busy. But, not too busy to be a mom, I mean. Oh God!"

"Alright then ma'am. Mrs. Jackson, I would just ask that you and Mr. Jackson come by my office tomorrow to sign the final paperwork. You will need to sign your son's name that you will legally give to the child. I assume you have a name. Can you stop by our office tomorrow then?"

Leona was rambling on and on about dates and names and finally was able to get out her response. "Yes! We can be there around 10:00am if that is okay."

Leona knew Tucker was at the house today, so she got home as quickly as possible. She ran into the house and found Tucker napping on the couch. Leona jumped onto her husband and nearly knocked his breath out and she grabbed him up into her arms and said, "hello daddy"!

Tucker looked at his wife with bug eyes and wasn't sure what was happening. "What did you say dear? Did you just call me daddy?" "Are you okay?"

"I am better than okay. I am a mommy! Our baby is here! Now! Today!" Leona was crying now and shaking. She explained the phone call and was rambling on when Tucker grabbed her tight and said, "are you certain?"

"Did you get that right? We are really getting a baby in a few days?"

"Yep! And guess what. It is a boy! You have a son Tucker Jackson. And we must sign for him tomorrow and give him a name."

The happy couple sat for another hour talking about the timing of all of this. They then decided to share the news with the team of friends that had stood by them all this time. But after further consideration they thought it best to let the election day happen and see where that took them. And then, they could share the news with everyone and bring baby Jackson home.

It was two days until election day. Anastasia and Hank invited the team for dinner. It was just their little group of friends but did include Abby's mother and Mark Hunter since they were part of the team now. They brought the baby and she slept most of the evening. Mark and Susan James talked all evening about antiques and art.

Noah had a grand re-opening of the art institute after some renovations had taken place. He gave everyone at dinner a ticket to the private event that would happen in February.

Chad also had great news as his full ownership of the Harley Davidson Motorcycle shop was official.

He too was having a kind of grand opening next week. To celebrate he brought black leather jackets with the name of his shop on the back and handed them out to each person at dinner. Even Susan and Mark got a jacket. The team was thrilled, and they took some photos posed in their Harley jackets gathered around the grand staircase of the Watkins home.

"This would be a great photo for the front page of the Post, should I win the Presidency!", said Anastasia. The group of friends laughed at the thought of it.

All the friends were coordinating dates on their phone calendars for the various events. Anastasia looked around the room and she could not be happier to be surrounded by such a wonderful group of people. She was pondering how she had gotten here and the mishaps along the way, and wondered if it was all worth it. She was sure that it was. Her team was so formidable and the movement of women around the country that managed to support her along the way was more than amazing. It gave her such empowerment. These people trusted her. They believed in her and what she stood for. They followed her for so many years on this journey. Could it really be happening, she thought. Will I be the next US President in a few days? Am I up to the task?

Anastasia held up a glass and got the attention of her guests. She gave a loving speech and mentioned each of them by name and had loving things to say about everything they had done to support her along the way.

Hank made his own toast to his lovely wife and thanked the group of friends for all they had done.

"It has taken us a few years to get here my friends. I think we can all agree that my wife is impressive!"

The group cheered and there were hugs and kisses and along with the happiness and joy there was a melancholy to the evening. This was either the beginning of something great or perhaps the end. They each could feel the sense of dread and the pondering of what their life would look like after the election if Anastasia did not win. But the group stood fast in their belief that tomorrow was going to be a great day. They had each other and they had wonderful, fulfilled lives. They separately shared looks and grins and more hugs than usual.

The evening ended with full stomachs and filled hearts. They said goodnight. Everyone will be taking the day off work tomorrow. Then on election day they would meet at the local Art Institute with the rest of the campaign volunteers and supporters and await the election results.

CHAPTER TWENTY-THREE

The day has arrived. Tucker and Leona were up all night with the new baby. They spent the entire day yesterday signing paperwork, setting up a crib, and gathering formula and other essentials for their new son. They always knew this day may come, and it would be a fire drill to get ready. They had a nursery set up about a year ago but because of all the delays they had stored most of the items and put the crib in the closet so they could use the space as an office.

Well, here they were now. Parents of a beautiful baby boy. And it is election day! The new parents could not get over the timing of all of this.

Tucker could be the new Vice President after the vote tonight. Their lives are going to be crazy busy, but the pair were just too happy to care about any of it. They would figure it all out. They had joked yesterday about their choice for the baby's name, and they loved their decision. They could not wait to share the news with Anastasia and the rest of the gang, and the plan was to do that tonight. Tucker felt bad about leaving but he had to meet up with Anastasia to show their united front for reporters that were gathering at the Art Institute with the rest of the campaign teams.

The polls opened and it did not take long for the numbers to begin rolling out on every television set in America. The news was broadcasting higher than ever votes cast by 2:00pm. The most votes "ever in history" for any US election.

News stories around the US showed huge crowds and particularly those with *Watkins for President* signs and signs that said, "*Gray-Haired Women of America for Watkins*". Yes, the Gray-Haired ladies showed up in mass to make their voices heard. Signs carried around Washington said, "Women Stand Up" and "Watkins is our Lady" and the best one according to Anastasia said, "*It Is Our Time – Watkins for President*".

By 7:00pm the news was reporting only Governor Jameson and Anastasia Watkins remained in the race and Watkins was leading by enough votes that they were calling for Jameson to just concede. But he hung on for another hour until it was obvious to everyone in the US and around the globe that Jameson was done. Watkins was leading by more than three hundred thousand votes. All the records were shattered for the most votes ever and for the most votes for one candidate ever.

Anastasia also broke other records. She would be the first ever woman president. She was the youngest President, and she had the support of more men and independent voters than ever before.

The group gathered in the massive lobby of the Art Institute and listened as Jameson conceded to Watkins. The crowd was going crazy inside the building and out on the streets. Across America people were celebrating more than in any other presidential election. It was time for change and for the US to move forward. Fireworks were going off in every state. Even the people of Mexas celebrated and hoped to be part of the US again someday.

The Watkins team had all gathered now. They were in a private suite and had been watching together all evening. The phone call came from Jameson and Anastasia silenced the group.

"Yes Robert. I appreciate that. Of course. You too. Thank you very much." Anastasia hung up the phone and screamed across the room. "We did it!" "Thank you!"

Just then as everyone was celebrating and the champagne corks were popping, Leona walked into the room holding their baby boy. Tucker had made some kind of excuse as to why she had not been there earlier. Everyone was silent for a moment and just stared at the pair.

Tucker smiled at Leona, and he announced to the group, "I want you to meet our son. Andrew Philip Jackson."

Anastasia smiled a huge smile and said, "Andrew Jackson!" And the rest of the friends began to laugh and hug Leona.

"We thought a presidential name would be appropriate considering the timing of everything", said Leona.

"Congratulations Madam President", said Kendall.

"Yes, cheers to OUR president!", said Abby and Noah.

The group was so happy, and their lives were so full. They had such admiration for one another and there was so much love in the room. Leona looked at little Andrew and her heart was so full. She looked into the eyes of her husband, and she gave him a kiss. "Now you go out there and show the world what a kick ass Vice President you are going to be!"

Withing the hour the team had assembled on stage behind the giant curtain that separated them from the roaring crowd on the other side. It was time. They had done it.

The music played and the curtain opened, and the team of friends saw the faces of all the beautiful people in front of them. These are our people, they thought. We are their people. They shared glances at one another, and they joined hands as Tucker and Anastasia stepped to the front of the line with arms intertwined and raised high.

"Hello America! Thank you so much. I am happy to accept your request to be your new president! It is a great day to be an American and an especially great day to be a woman in America!" "Thank you, ladies!!" "We did it!"

The music roared and the balloons dropped, and confetti spilled out across the crowded ballroom. It was 2052 and it certainly was a great day to be a woman, Leona thought. And now a mother. It is going to be a great year!

THE END

A note from the author –

I did not set out to write a political story. I got this idea about the older women, like me, in America and what we are going through now. Then when I began to think about what I hoped for my future and for the future of my grandchildren, the story just came pouring out of me.

I hope our future is bright and I hope in my lifetime I do see a woman in the oval office as my President. It will happen. All of us gray-haired ladies need to stick together and never give up the fight for our rights.

I hope you enjoyed this story, and it gives you hope!

Cindy

Check out these other books written and published by Cynthia Blanton:

Trilogy - The Redlake Series

MURDER AT REDLAKE

ESCAPE FROM REDLAKE

SEASIDE SERENITY

Documentary - STRONG WOMEN

Latest Book -   THE END OF FOREVER

Current Book - The Secret Society of Gray-Haired Women

Cynthia Blanton, Author – Facebook Page

Find all my books on Amazon.com / Kindle Direct Publishing (E-Book; Paperback; Hardcover)